*Studies in Victorian Life
and Literature*

Thomas Carlyle. Watercolor by Simeon Solomon. Courtesy of Special Collections, University Library, University of California, Santa Cruz.

Carlyle *and the* *Search for* *Authority*

Chris R. Vanden Bossche

Ohio State University Press
Columbus

Library of Congress Cataloging-in-Publication Data
Vanden Bossche, Chris R.
Carlyle and the search for authority / Chris R. Vanden Bossche.
p.   cm. — (Studies in Victorian life and literature)
Includes bibliographical references and index.
ISBN 0–8142–0538–0 (alk. paper)
1. Carlyle, Thomas, 1795–1881—Criticism and interpretation.
2. Authority in literature.
I. Title.   II. Series.
PR4437.A89V36   1991
824'.8—dc20   90–44890
CIP

Printed in the U.S.A.

9 8 7 6 5 4 3 2 1

Contents

Preface

"PLEASE GOD WE shall begin ere long to love art for art's sake," Thackeray wrote in 1839. "It is Carlyle who has worked more than any other to give it its independence" (1:396). It is easy to forget that Carlyle was the contemporary of Shelley and Keats—Thackeray was reviewing the *Critical and Miscellaneous Essays*, which had just recently been published but contained material dating back to 1827—that he belonged to the generation of Romantic artists who attempted to make art a religion, a discourse with a visionary and transcendental status. They did so, as Raymond Williams argued, because they hoped to find in art an authority for "certain human values, capacities, energies, which the development of society towards an industrial civilization was felt to be threatening or destroying" (*Culture and Society*, 36; see Lentricchia, 5–8; Graff, 28–34, 90–96). They claimed that art alone could provide the values they felt were absent from or even destroyed by newly dominant discourses like political economy. The problem with this view, as Williams and others have argued, is that, by elevating art, by attempting to give it its "independence," these writers tended to separate it from everyday social life. Because artists insisted that literary discourse was of a different order than the discourse of political economy (or science, or sociology, and so on), they undermined artistic authority; the public turned to political economy and its cognates when it wanted a representation of how society really works.

None of this would be of much concern to us if these writers had merely wanted to advocate a rigorous aestheticism, but the art for art's sake they promoted was meant to have social effects. Their intention in advocating art for art's sake was to insist that art did not exist merely for the sake of entertainment or pleasure, but had a more profound role to play; rather than removing art from society, they were arguing that society could not exist without it. In the process, they raised art above other forms of discourse because they felt that only a transcendental discourse could author(ize) a just social order superior to that constructed in competing discourses. Nonetheless, this Romantic transcendentalism, and the literary formalism that evolved from it, are, as has often been noted, at odds with the Romantic desire to intervene in the political world because it removes art and the artist from the historical processes of social formation. By raising the artist *above* society, this view of art brought into question the artist's ability to act *in* society.

Thomas Carlyle occupies a unique position among nineteenth-century artists and critics because he was early drawn to transcendental aestheticism and then was among the first to recognize its dangers. Indeed, by the time Thackeray was depicting him as the leading spokesman of the aesthetic school, he had already abandoned it and was advising poets to take up some other line of work. Yet, as he turned to history and politics, Carlyle did not leave behind his transcendentalism. Like his contemporaries, he felt that the discourses to which he was opposed led to an ethical relativism that could only be cured by recourse to transcendental authority. This insistence on a transcendental source of authority is crucial to understanding why the artists who mounted the most powerful critiques of emerging industrial capitalism were nonetheless much more politically conservative than those writing in other modes of discourse. Instead of abandoning the transcendentalism of his early writings and seeking to discover how communal values might be constructed through the sociohistorical processes of cultural formation, Carlyle transformed his aesthetic transcendentalism into a political authoritarianism that he regarded as the sole means of counteracting the destruction of values and social cohesion by the emerging industrial order. In order to understand Carlyle and his contemporaries, we must understand why their discourse seemed to allow only two alternatives: the anarchy of a value-free society, on the one hand, or the social order and justice of an authoritarian state, on the other.

These questions have two implications for the study of Carlyle and his writings. First, if we are going to understand the relationship between his early faith in art and his later faith in political authority, it will be necessary to examine his entire literary career. Although it is often rightly asserted that all of the later Carlyle can be found in the earlier Carlyle, it is nonetheless the fact that the later, more disturbing, Carlyle has received relatively scant attention.[1] Consequently, because we are unable to see exactly what the relationship between early and late is, we fail to understand the precise nature of the problems in the early Carlyle or what really happens in the later works. Second, because this study is concerned with the danger of treating art as something that exists outside of history and society, it examines Carlyle's writings in relation to the development of his career as a writer and to the audiences for which he wrote. It was once necessary to rescue Victorian writers from a treatment that considered their ideas in isolation from their art, but if we go too far in the other direction we are in danger of treating them only as artists, not as social thinkers. Of course, it is the distinction between art and ideas itself that is pernicious, and Carlyle's best critics have always recognized that his writings are the work of a master rhetorician. This study attempts to extend their insights by combining an analysis of his rhetorical technique with an understanding of the rhetorical contexts in which he wrote, the immediate concerns, both private and public, to which his works were addressed.

I will begin with a discussion, in chapter 1, of the historical development of what Carlyle and his contemporaries regarded as a crisis of authority. I will then proceed, in chapter 2, to examine how Carlyle constructed his literary career as an attempt to establish a new mode of authority that would replace the religious vocation prescribed by his father. The following chapters (3 through 6) will investigate the history of his struggles to discover authority in the succeeding phases of his career: his exploration of the dialectic of revolution and authority, his failed attempt to author a new social order, the return of the theme of paternal authority, and, finally, the end of writing that brought him no closer to solving the dilemma of literature. This analysis assumes that in our own era, in which the advocates of literature continue to assert its unique value in the face of much public indifference, we can still learn a good deal about this predicament by studying how it took shape in the writings of authors like Carlyle. At the same time, we need to keep in mind that if Carlyle helped create this dilemma, he did so in earnest; he recognized a problem—a problem that still seems very real to us—and thought he saw in art the best means of addressing it. It is to be hoped that by examining his failures, we can better understand our own failures and perhaps begin to find our own solutions.

Research for this study was partially funded by travel grants from the National Endowment for the Humanities and the Jesse Jones Foundation. I also received frequent assistance from the department of special collections at the University of California, Santa Cruz, which houses the Norman and Charlotte Strouse Carlyle Collection. The wording of a few sentences and the substance of several passages of this book are drawn from essays on Carlyle that I have published in *The Carlyle Newsletter, Prose Studies, The Journal of Narrative Technique, Dickens Studies Annual,* and *The Arnoldian.* I thank the editors of these journals for their permission to reproduce this material. While I have acknowledged direct borrowings in my notes, I owe a debt to the Carlyle scholarship and criticism of the past three decades that far exceeds what is acknowledged there. I would especially single out the editors of the Duke edition of the Carlyle letters, whose comprehensive, excellently annotated and indexed edition has saved me a great deal of work and greatly enhanced the final product.

Many individuals have been helpful along the way, both reading earlier versions of this study and discussing the questions involved. I thank especially many colleagues and students at the University of California, Santa Cruz, and the University of Notre Dame, as well as the editors of the Essential Carlyle. Among these, I want to express my special gratitude to Murray Baumgarten, whose fine ambivalence toward Carlyle is, I hope, given ample expression in this book. Above all, I want to thank my most valued accomplice in criticism, Laura Haigwood.

ONE

Introduction: The Crisis of Authority and the Critique of Political Economy

CARLYLE'S WORKS represent and attempt to resolve dilemmas raised by what he and his contemporaries perceived as a revolutionary shift of authority in virtually all realms of discourse and institutions of power in western Europe. From his vantage, it appeared not only that authority had shifted but that the transcendental grounds for it had been undermined. Empiricism and individual reason had replaced the discourses of tradition and transcendental revelation, and democratic and individualistic institutions had replaced hierarchical ones. Instead of originating in an absolute and transcendental source outside of society, the meaning of discourse and the legitimacy of power now appeared to derive from the system of relations that constituted society and its discourses (Foucault, chap. 8). Since authority authors and authorizes both discourses that ground social being—in the form of belief—and social relations that establish ethical principles—in the form of the law—both the meaning of beliefs and the justice of the law were affected by this shift.

Carlyle shared the anxiety of many of his contemporaries that a self-defining system—of signifiers, social relations, or beliefs—could not produce meaning, order, or ethical standards, that with no transcendental authority to guarantee meaning and value, the world becomes meaningless and lawless. Yet he believed that the revolutionary overturning of authority had become necessary: his writings turned again and again to the subject of revolution—the French Revolution, the English Revolution, the revolutions of 1830 and 1848, and the industrial revolution. By attempting to resolve the dialectic between revolution and authority, Carlyle sought both to establish his own authority and to recuperate authority in the social domain.

Carlyle and his contemporaries represented this shift in authority

1

as a crisis that arose from the dissolution of the theocratic government of the Middle Ages and its replacement by secular political economy. Like Burke and Coleridge before him, Carlyle was concerned with the rise of modern state capitalism and blamed its shortcomings on the separation of church and state as well as the destruction of religious and political authority. The remainder of this introductory chapter will review the debate on authority in the early modern period that gave rise to the critiques of Carlyle's predecessors, Burke and Coleridge—critiques that represented the history of the seventeenth and eighteenth centuries as a revolutionary crisis and dictated a return to theocracy as its solution.

Nineteenth-century writers frequently represented the governments of the Middle Ages as theocracies in which authority was both unitary and transcendental because it originated in the divine will. Authority, in this sense, can be seen as the ability to author definitive structures of belief and codes of behavior. Both in the papacy and in European monarchies, authority had been represented as moving down through a graduated hierarchy, from the divinity "on high" to pope or monarch, to aristocracy or episcopate, and finally to the people (Kern, 7; see Carter, 29–31; Brown, 70). Since all authority derived from divinity, the state could be considered a theocracy in which religious belief and social order had been ordained by a single transcendental source. The Reformation and the democratic revolution appeared to have destroyed the theocratic principle in favor of the separation of church and state. Once religion and polity were treated as separate institutions and discourses with their own internal principles, the necessity for their relationship disappeared and the separation of church and state ensued. At the same time, the locus of authority was shifting within both church and state.

The debate on religious authority revolved around the problem of revelation, the discourse of belief. By arguing that individuals could discern God's will by reading the Bible on their own, Protestants shifted authority from the church hierarchy to the ordinary believer, from a corporate body to individuals. The advance of this shift can be illustrated by sects like the Quakers, who sought to eliminate all mediation of the divine word by claiming that one does not even need the Bible to discover divine revelation; one need only look into one's heart. The higher criticism—which in the eighteenth century reinterpreted the Bible as a collection of myths that could only be interpreted through a knowledge of its history—further undermined biblical authority. By the nineteenth century, it appeared that each individual would become a sect unto himself or herself, spurring the proliferation of what Matthew Arnold was to call "hole-in-the-corner churches" (*Culture and Anarchy*, 28).[1]

What concerned Carlyle and other nineteenth-century critics was that this proliferation of private beliefs seemed less like the production of a new belief than the destruction of the old. It has become a commonplace of intellectual history that while the leaders of the Reformation did not challenge transcendental authority itself, since that would have contradicted their fundamental religious beliefs, their claim that no dogmatic revelation (of the Roman church) could be proven true and authoritative was a form of skepticism (Popkin, xix–xxi). Heterodox skeptics did not have far to go when, arguing that revelation was never consistent with reason, they denied the validity of revelation in favor of rational inquiry and empirical observation. The authority of discourse need no longer derive from the position of the speaker in the hierarchy or from tradition, but from its own internal consistency. Any belief authorized merely by tradition or by a member of the hierarchy could be considered a superstitious delusion. Carlyle's significance for the nineteenth century was, in part, that he was an heir both to the tradition of Protestant reform—the religion of his parents—and to Scottish skepticism—the intellectual milieu of the University of Edinburgh. The problem, as he saw it, was how to author a belief to replace the faith in which he could no longer believe.

During the same era, the authority of the hierarchical state was being challenged, and political discourse, like religious discourse, had begun to represent authority as vested in the individuals that constituted the state rather than in monarchical hierarchy. Seventeenth-century discourse on political authority was dominated by the debate between proponents of patriarchy and of social contract, the theory of patriarchy reaching its fullest articulation in response to the challenge from the theory of social contract.[2] Patriarchal theory—an extension and justification of the theory of divine right—drew an analogy between the absolute authority of the monarch over his kingdom and the absolute authority of the father over his family. Locke's refutation of Robert Filmer's *Patriarcha*—the fullest articulation of patriarchal theory—provided the first complete elaboration of the opposing theory of social contract. The authority of parents over their children, he pointed out, is not absolute, since it exists only during the period of their dependency. Parents cannot bind their children to a contract; instead, each child must, upon reaching adulthood, agree to a contract establishing the relationship between them. Similarly, each generation has consented, either implicitly or explicitly, to the contract that determines the relationship between the government and its citizens (*Two Treatises*, 363–64; see Schochet, 247–53). The authority of the contract derives not from divine ordination in the past, but from consent of the people in the present. Consequently, Locke argued that governors obtain their authority not through heredity—a divinely conferred ordination—but through individual merit, by choice of the "ablest" to govern (*Two Treatises*, 35; see Schochet, 266).[3]

The theory of contract had two significant consequences. First, it shifted authority to the people and to relationships among individuals in society. Second, it justified changes in social institutions, introducing the possibility of altering the contract each time it was renewed as opposed to assuming that a single inalterable institution had been created by the divine authorization of primal monarchy. If government did not uphold its obligations under the contract, the people might legitimately overthrow the government, an option precluded by the discourse of patriarchy (*Two Treatises*, 432–34).

The theory of social contract need not challenge monarchy, just as the insistence on individual conscience and reason need not challenge belief in God, but it does alter the grounds of political authority—the terms of the discourse in which it is discussed and the representation of its institutions—just as the Reformation altered the grounds of religious faith and the form of religious institutions. As long as authority was regarded as transcendental, it took on a hierarchical form, represented as emanating downward from a single central source "on high" into the social mass below. In the new discourse of the parliamentary ruling class, hierarchy tended to disappear, as government became representative of, rather than superior to, the people (Bendix, 318–19; Pitkin, Intro.). The same skeptics who dismissed revelation and orthodox belief in favor of reason and empiricism could easily extend the theory of social contract to dismiss monarchy in favor of representational democracy. When authority became a matter of the internal consistency of a discourse rather than imposition from above or outside, law and social order became a matter of establishing the principles that were to govern relationships among individuals—a social contract—rather than a natural order (like the family) imposed by an external authority. Nineteenth-century critics of democracy were concerned that under such circumstances there was no certain way of finding an "ablest" to govern the state, and they consequently revived the patriarchal or paternalistic argument that there could be no social order that is not, to some degree, a hierarchical order of governors and governed (D. Roberts, passim).

These changes in the political organization of the state coincided with changes in its economic organization, the rise of democracy co-inciding with the emergence of modern state capitalism. Society was understood as a series of contracts among competing individuals instead of a corporate body united as a single family.

It is no coincidence that the metaphor used to articulate the new representation of polity—the contract—was borrowed from the discourse of economy. As the metaphor for government shifted from family to contract, the word *economy* came to designate the workings of the larger system of the polity rather than the management of a household; it was only at this time that economy emerged as a distinct discourse that could become the foundation for other discourses (Galbraith, 31 passim). Rationality itself came to be considered in terms of economy as the internal constitution and apportionment of functions within a particular realm, including the principle that discourses and institutions are self-consistent systems (MacIntyre, 25; see Brown, 71–72; Graff, 41).

As the urban middle class began to assume political power, it asserted itself through a reorganization of the socioeconomic realm. In the eighteenth century, Parliament, as representative of individual property owners, took control of governmental finance, effecting a shift from an economy regulated by royal authority to a laissez-faire economy that favored the interests of the individual (Bendix, 307). At the same time, Adam Smith's *Wealth of Nations* codified the discourse of political economy as a self-sufficient system isolated from social ends. Smith's opening discussion of the division of labor established the principle of economic production by discrete, isolated, and interchangeable persons, depicting the nation as a collectivity of free individuals—merchants competing to sell their goods and laborers competing to sell their labor—in a self-regulating and self-enclosed system. Principles of value, justice, or fairness, it was argued, could not be guaranteed by the intervention of a divinely authorized government because that government was external to the self-sufficient economic system; such principles must evolve from within the economic system of self-interest. Ethics had become a function of the system rather than a belief according to which it operated.

Proponents of Smith's doctrine were, generally speaking, advocates for increased democracy; and, conversely, critics of the industrial economy tended to be defenders of the old political order as well as supporters of established religion. What concerned the latter, in economics as in politics and religion, was the absence of any higher authority to which one could appeal on questions of justice and the fear that the old hierarchy, which they identified with chivalric ideals of justice, was being replaced by a new elite that was concerned only with pursuing its own private interests. It seemed that theocracy as a system that transmitted religious belief into social practice had been replaced by political economy in which belief was effaced by self-interest, that theocracy had given way to an anarchic battle for individual dominance.

As the discourse of authority was changing during this era, the authority of discourse could not be unaffected, and these representations of the movement from theocracy to political economy found a parallel in representations of language. The representation of money, to which words had long been compared, altered along with changes in political economy (see Shell, 1–11). Under monarchy, only heads of state had the authority to coin money because the value of coins was guaranteed, or authorized, by them; conversely, the ability to coin money could be used by rulers to establish their authority (Galbraith, 28–29). The phrase "the king's English" implied a similar royal prerogative with respect to language (the *OED* comments that the expression was apparently "suggested by phrases like 'to deface the king's coin'"). In the modern era, the grounds of meaning and value, of language and money, shifted from monarchical authorization to the internal organization of the monetary and linguistic systems. Like religion, polity, and economy, language and money became self-enclosed systems; meaning and value were determined by historical relationships within the linguistic and monetary systems, not by reference to an external authority. When banknotes appeared in the seventeenth century and the first paper currency in the eighteenth, their value was guaranteed by the gold they represented and for which they could be exchanged at any time. But since the value of these bills depended as much on the authority of the inscriptions vouching for their authenticity as on the gold they represented, it became apparent that money would retain its value as long as people were willing to exchange it at a relatively fixed rate (Morgan, 19, 21–22). Accordingly, in the nineteenth century, currencies that were not convertible to precious metal were first introduced.

Such currencies correspond to semiotic representations of language as a system in which signifiers obtain their meaning through their relationships with one another—as, in the monetary system, money gains value—and not in relationship to a signified—or money backed by gold. The representation of languages as internally consistent systems by twentieth-century linguistics was already implicit in the historical linguistics of the previous century and a half. The principle that meaning can only be determined by examining words in context, the principle of historical philology, implied that language gains its meaning by reference to itself, not to some authority outside of itself. In political economy, the individual became free, not to create money, but to create value that could be translated into money. In the domain of language, the individual became free to create meaning. As in the other areas, these changes created anxieties, in this case about the validity of language and the ability to create and control meaning. Misusing the king's English, altering its meaning, was to make valueless words; individuals who coined their own words could be regarded as counterfeiters who upset the social hierarchy by violating the decorum of language as established by the aristocracy.

These anxieties about linguistic production cannot be separated from major changes in literary production. Like "political economy," which appeared in the early modern era, the domain of "literature" arose only in the nineteenth century.[4] The patronage system—which gave considerable control over the production of writing to the upper classes who supported authors—reinforced the idea that the aristocracy controlled linguistic coinage, while the emergence of the literate middle class in the eighteenth century gave rise to the bookseller system, in which authors were supported by the profits on sales of books that were now commercial commodities (Kernan, chap. 2). As the market of literate readers widened, authors were "freed" to produce texts for any segment of it they chose. The opening decades of the century saw the founding of the Whig *Edinburgh Review,* followed by the Tory *Quarterly Review,* the philosophic radicals' *London and Westminster Review,* and hundreds of other periodicals and newspapers representing every social and political faction. As opposed to the patronage system, in which writers were authorized to promulgate the views of a unitary hierarchy, the bookseller system enabled authors to represent hundreds of individual social factions, so literature became "a locus of political contention rather than a terrain of cultural consensus" (Eagleton, 39). Literary texts no longer reflected hierarchical authority but the demands of the popular market.

Yet nineteenth-century representations of literature frequently contradicted this fact of the marketplace, depicting the writer as a visionary free from its constraints. Rather than representing literature as part of the new social order dominated by political economy, the critics of political economy would represent it as an alternative to commerce. The immense explosion of print in the nineteenth century meant that an author could directly reach an enormous audience compared to those available in previous centuries. A writer like Carlyle had the potential for enormous influence, and there is little doubt that his writings did, in many ways—both positive and negative—have a tremendous impact on his contemporaries. But the fact that buyers in the marketplace decided what would be read meant that his was always only one of many contending voices. Although writers had been freed to create their own systems of meaning, this artistic freedom was at odds with the determinations of the marketplace. This study will consequently concern itself with why Carlyle's career as a man of letters was largely a career of frustration.

Carlyle, Burke, and Coleridge belong to the tradition identified in Raymond Williams's *Culture and Society* as providing a critique of political economy while at the same time creating problematic alternatives—in part, it may be argued, because they accepted some of political economy's fundamental premises. At the beginning of the nineteenth century, it appeared to Carlyle's predecessors that England and Europe had abandoned theocracy in favor of political economy, and they developed the analysis of political economy that represented this historical change not merely as a shift of authority but as the destruction of it. Their representations of historical change expressed their anxiety that the absence of transcendental authority meant the absence of *any* kind of authority or social order, that neither belief nor law, neither order nor justice could exist if social institutions were only self-enclosed systems. The idyll of theocracy and patriarchy, they concluded, had given way to the warfare of political economy. Carlyle, like Burke and Coleridge before him, longed to return to that prelapsarian idyll; yet, while he extended Burke's and Coleridge's critique of political economy, he did not share their belief that the religious and political institutions of the past could serve the present. Consequently, his writings manifest, in a particularly acute form, the Victorian desire both to recapture the transcendental idyll and to remain on the battlefield of history.

The ideal of theocracy underlies both Burke's and Coleridge's defenses of the union of church and state, of the church establishment and the British constitution. Burke's *Reflections on the Revolution* was prompted no less by his antipathy for the atheism of the revolutionaries than by his distrust of their politics (xv, xxii). He argued that since religion was the basis of civil society, the French were undermining the social order when they rejected religion and the established church (43, 102–9, 113). Political authorities, he wrote, "stand in the person of God," holding "power" only insofar as they "act in trust" for the nation and are accountable to the "Author, and Founder of Society"; without religion, power is unbounded and corruption follows (105–6). Like Burke, Coleridge, who sustained an interest in the relationship between church and state from the 1790s to the publication of *On the Constitution of the Church and State* in 1830, argued that the church should check the abuse of political power (xl, 51).[5]

Both Burke and Coleridge were concerned that the rise of commerce was encouraging the dissolution of church and state. Throughout his analysis of the revolution, Burke used the worthless paper currency, the *assignat,* as a symbol for the moral emptiness of the revolutionary government (273–75; see also 44, 60, 62). He also contrasted the genuine social "contract" that constitutes the "state" with commercial contracts that are "temporary and perishable," arguing that the proper contract is "but a clause in the great primeval contract of eternal society, linking the lower with the higher natures, connecting the visible and invisible world, according to a fixed compact" (110). He thus reverted to an earlier form of contract theory in which the contract made by the first generation remains binding on succeeding generations, as opposed to Locke's contract, which is renewed by each generation and can be dissolved in appropriate circumstances. The association of the revolutionary government with the valueless *assignat* and the temporary contract both implied that the government was not, as it should be, authorized by a higher authority. Not surprisingly, Burke feared that the false "worship" of "trade and manufacture, the gods of our economical politicians" would lead to an equally disastrous revolution in England (90). Coleridge similarly argued that the state should counterbalance the commercial spirit and that the landed gentry should not be involved in commerce, since their role was to hold their land "in trust" for the nation (*Constitution*, 51; *Sermons*, 223, see also 170–94, 223–29). Although Burke was aware that the age of chivalry was dead, and Coleridge that the landed aristocracy was learning to treat its land not as a trust for the nation but as a commercial commodity, both writers insisted that the commercial middle class must be held in check by an ethical discourse like chivalry or Christianity, and by the institutions of the landed aristocracy and the Anglican church (*Reflections*, 87; *Sermons*, 141–49).

Carlyle would join Burke and Coleridge in their critique of middle-class democracy and shared their longing for a return to hierarchical authority. He, too, understood that rationality had come under the dominion of economy, arguing as early as "Signs of the Times" (1829) that political economy was becoming the model for all discourses and institutions. "Signs of the Times" claimed that the requirement that institutions and discourse be rationalized by efficiency, profit, and utility coincided with the dismissal of the requirement that they possess meaningfulness or value, in other words, that Smith, De Lolme, and Bentham had substituted a mechanical system—the "physical, practical, *economical* condition, as regulated by public laws"—for one concerned with "the moral, religious, spiritual condition of the people" (*CME*, 2:67; emphasis added). Carlyle argued further that principles of freedom and individual liberty encouraged the economic individualism that atomized the nation and destroyed social responsibility, replacing the Christian gospel with a mechanistic gospel of profit and loss (*CME*, 2:60–61).[6] Insisting that social order can exist only through transcendental authority, he concluded that the gospel of profit and loss would never produce the equivalent of the moral order implicit in the Crusades, the Reformation, or the English Revolution (*CME*, 2:71).

The fundamentals of this critique of political economy underlay nearly all of Carlyle's subsequent social criticism, but he constantly reformulated it in his search for authority. While he shared Burke's and Coleridge's belief that the restoration of authority required a restoration of hierarchy, he did not share their view that this restoration could occur through returning power to the existing landed aristocracy. As a dissenter and a Scotsman from the artisan class, he regarded the Church of England and the aristocracy as corrupt and hopelessly outmoded (a single aristocrat, he calculated, ate the fruit of "6,666 men's labour" and only killed partridges in return [*TNB*, 159–60]). Although he shared many assumptions of the would-be revivers of patriarchalism, he also shared the Enlightenment assumptions underlying the theory of the social contract. Whereas Burke and Coleridge sought a return from revolution to authority, Carlyle sought a return to authority through revolution.

The key issue in nineteenth-century discourse on authority was, indeed, whether revolution destroys or restores authority. The French Revolution, which seemed to epitomize and concentrate in its short history the whole history of shifting authority that had been taking place over the past few centuries, became the type of all revolutions, the ground where one tested one's position on revolution. What distinguished Carlyle's contribution to this debate was that, while he was an heir to the conservative tradition of Burke and Coleridge that represented revolution as the destruction of authority, he combined this tradition with a more radical one that represented revolution as a search for and means of recovering authority.

Burke's opposition to the French Revolution derived in large part from his particular conception of authority and social change. His depiction of the British constitution as an evolving set of institutions and social practices underlay his argument that the state must be able to change in order to conserve itself. Thus he did not oppose change, but his use of the term "conservation" made explicit his view of change as a return to the principles of the constitution (24). Authority resided neither in the divine right of the monarch nor in electoral franchise, but in the constitution regarded as the accumulation of traditional wisdom about political governance (29–30). Whereas Burkean conservatism would preserve the constitution, revolution was the "solution [i. e., dissolution] of continuity" provided by it (20). From Burke's perspective, the Jacobin constitution had no authority because it was created ex nihilo by a small group of middle-class lawyers and was completely cut off from the existing social order. Burke implied that the authors of the English constitution were disinterested because its creation had transcended the lives and specific interests of any particular group of men, while the French constitution was limited to the vision of a special-interest group. Like Burke's British constitution, Coleridge's "statesman's manual" (the Bible) would provide a ground for religious and political institutions, and he opposed it to the abstract, theoretical speculations of political scientists, which are limited by the human understanding (*Sermons*, 31). Both Burke and Coleridge, like Arnold later, opposed "Jacobinism" because they believed that it substituted abstractions—by which they meant a conception of society as a self-enclosed system—for the concrete plenitude of the British constitution grounded in transcendental authority (*Reflections*, 46–47, 69; *Sermons*, 28–32, 63).

Carlyle would concur that political order and religious belief must be grounded in divine justice and truth, but he would favor revolution nonetheless, not because it aimed to create a new constitution or sacred text, but because it destroyed the old. Burke's and Carlyle's views of the English Revolution manifest the difference in their orientation. For Burke, the English Revolution was the glorious revolution of 1688. Its aim, he argued, was not to do away with the old order, but to preserve the ancient constitution that was being undermined by James II (35ff.). Carlyle, on the other hand, sympathized with the Puritans and the revolution of 1640 which, like the French Revolution, committed regicide, the symbolic destruction of monarchy and the established order. In his view, the Puritans had acted in the name of God, attempting to reestablish society on the basis of divine law rather than the principles of the constitution.[7]

Burke and Coleridge assumed that existing discourses and institutions still possessed authority and could be reinvigorated, whereas Carlyle thought they had become empty forms. In the case of the French Revolution, Carlyle, like Burke, complained that in destroying the old order the French had not created a new one; but, unlike Burke, he thought that the destruction of the old order was necessary. The French Revolution, he was to argue early on, was not the cause of change, but a product of the deep need for change. "All Europe is in a state of disturbance, of Revolution" and the "whole frame of Society is rotten," he insisted; it "must go for fuel-wood" (*TNB*, 184; see

CME, 2:82). Whereas Burke depicted existing institutions as flexible and able to evolve, Carlyle represented them as rotten and hollow, a "thin rind of Habit" that no longer embodied authority (*CL*, 6:302; see *CL*, 6:52). In both instances, he rejected the text—Burke's British constitution and Coleridge's statesman's manual—through which his predecessors had authorized the status quo, and sought instead to discover the authority that could author a new text and new institutions.

As we shall see, Carlyle regarded the French Revolution as necessary and was remarkably approving in his representation of it, but he also saw it merely as the means to an end, as the necessary destruction of the old order preliminary to a creation of the new. It could destroy outworn authority, but it possessed no authority of its own, nor could it establish authority. For Carlyle the revolution was still taking place; it had annihilated the old order, but the authority to create a new order had not yet been discovered. The restoration of authority that he advocated challenged emerging middle-class democracy but would also be challenged and rejected by it.

Consequently, his lifelong search for authority was endless. Part of the problem lay in the ambiguous concept of authority itself. Historically, authority has two basic denotations: (1) the power or right to enforce obedience; (2) the power or right to influence or inspire belief. Yet the adjectives that correspond to these two forms of authority, "authoritative" and "authoritarian," have opposing honorific and pejorative connotations (Carter, 7). The authoritative and authoritarian tend to be aligned with belief and the law, respectively. When a society's belief does not correspond to the law, the society experiences the law not as authoritative, but as authoritarian. Such a society will rebel in the name of an authority with which it seeks to merge so as to avoid alienation in the law external to itself. But, from another point of view, society comes to regard this new belief as equally false because it is specific to the rebelling faction, it is not authoritative. In the name of society at large, society suppresses the rebellious faction, which again is moved to rebel against the law. The cyclic alternation between rebellion and suppression constitutes, for Carlyle, the fundamental course of history. The theocratic idyll in which law is coextensive with belief exists only in a moment of transcendence that is antithetical to the historical cycle in which belief and the law alternate. While Carlyle depicts all beliefs and laws as representations that are necessarily historical, he longs to return to and make permanent the theoretical moment when those representations coincide with the transcendental, and so escape history.[8]

Carlyle's search for authority first led him to the German Romantics, who depicted the man of letters as capable of assuming the authority to recover the theocratic idyll. His attempts to imagine and represent the recuperation of authority would encounter and struggle with the problems that arise from trying to make literature and the author transcendentally authoritative. He was to anticipate later critics in discovering that the Romantic religion of art, far from recovering the transcendental and escaping individualism, merely intensified interiority. This problem led him, in the latter part of his career, to seek the recovery of authority in the hero as king. Yet even as Carlyle moved away from privileging the authority of the man of letters, he did not personally abandon literature—that is to say, he did not quit writing. By continuing to write from a perspective that assumed the transcendental authority of literature, he both enabled a profound critique of Victorian society and disabled literature as a force within that society. In the process of establishing and asserting his own authority and seeking the grounds of social authority, he enacted the dilemma of literature.

TWO

Becoming an Author:
1820–1830

"IN ONE OF these families, in a house which his father, who was a mason, had built with his own hands, Thomas Carlyle was born on December 4, 1795" (*EL*, 1:3). These biographical facts represented for Carlyle the place and time that constituted him as rebel and author. The house symbolized his birth into a community created by and embodied in its builder and chief authority, James Carlyle. Seventeen ninety-five, significantly, was the year with which Carlyle was to conclude his history of the French Revolution. He was born into both a timeless space in which authority and belief had not yet become problematic, and a world fraught with historical time as manifested in the revolutionary upheavals that culminated a century of skepticism and inaugurated an "Era of Unbelief" (*SR*, 112).

This birth into the conflicting realms of authority and revolution provided the terms of the narrative through which Carlyle represented his literary career. In the 1820s, he created a series of narratives describing the process of becoming an author. Through these biographical, fictional, and autobiographical narratives—which reached their climax in the narrative of Diogenes Teufelsdröckh's discovery of his vocation as author in *Sartor Resartus*—Carlyle strove to make himself both author and authority.[1]

Schiller, Goethe, and the Career Narrative

The revivers of the patriarchal theory of government in the early nineteenth century regarded the history of the family unit as a microcosm of the larger historical movement from theocratic patriarchy to social contract. Significantly, those writers like Burke and Coleridge who

15

wished to return to the theocratic idyll also helped to revive patriarchal theory (which had waned in the eighteenth century), making
the family the model of hierarchical and communal harmony in opposition to the warfare inherent in economic individualism (Schochet,
276–81; D. Roberts, 17–32). Carlyle's portrayal of the career of the
man of letters borrows from this tradition the narrative exile from and
return to the idyllic family.

We can see the critique of the national shift from theocracy to political economy being applied to the history of the family in Peter Gaskell's
Artisans and Machinery (1833), which represents the destruction of an
idyllic family by the urban factory system.[2] In Gaskell's narrative, the
home of the preindustrial family comprises a harmonious domestic
economy to which each family member makes a contribution; because
they work together, they do not have "separate and distinct" interests
but share communal aims (60). The relationship between parents and
children is a benign hierarchy in which "parental authority" guides
children in their moral development (59). The urban economy, in
which members of the family no longer work together at home but in
separate factories or different parts of a factory, destroys this unity:
as individual family members earn their own wages, they no longer
hold a common interest in the profits of their labor. In fact, conflicting
interests divide the family, and "quarrelling, fighting, a total alienation
of affection, and finally, a separation from home" ensue (88; see 68).
Correspondingly, urban factory life upsets the hierarchical relations
between parents and children and undermines the moral influence
of parents promoted by those relations: once they become financially
independent, children are no longer compelled to obey their parents (64, 85–87). When "selfishness" replaces "Sacred obligations,"
the home becomes a mere "lodging-house" in which the members of
the family are related to one another only by "pecuniary profit and
loss" (65).

Gaskell's narrative suggests that the industrial system does not possess any means of producing a moral code or a just social order. On
the contrary, he argues, in addition to destroying the moral influence
of parents, the factory system itself promotes immorality. Although
he does not offer specific solutions, Gaskell's critique of the industrial
"revolution" implies the necessity of introducing the familial community of interest into the urban economy by recovering the domestic
idyll of a preindustrial era (362).

Carlyle's Schiller and Goethe recuperate the domestic idyll by turning to the institution of literature. In Carlyle's first book, *The Life of Schiller* (1823–25), the young Schiller wants to become a clergyman, but the duke of Würtemberg convinces his father to place him in a military college and make him study the law, which becomes "representative," for Schiller, of the restraints of education by "military drill" (10, 9). Schiller's desire for a higher calling beyond the limits of the law brings him into conflict with the authoritarian father figure, the duke. Unable to pursue his theological interests, he begins to read and write poetry. His first play, *The Robbers*, thematically enacts his rebellion against the authority of the duke while seeking to establish his own authority as an artist. The duke, recognizing the challenge to his authority, condemns *The Robbers* as a dangerous work and threatens Schiller with further repression. But when becoming a successful author frees Schiller "from school tyranny and military constraint," he rejects his prescribed career, flees Würtemberg, and establishes himself as a man of letters (24).

Since he has no religious doubts, Schiller does not, unlike Carlyle's other heroes who replace a religious with a literary career, reject the religious beliefs of his own father. But by rebelling against the father figure, the duke, he is effectively exiled from the "religious" idyll of the family, which disappears from the biography after he leaves Würtemberg. Precisely because he does not lose his religious faith, Schiller's exile makes his career in literature problematic. Literature does not enable him to return home because it cannot fully replace what it does not fully reject. He becomes a "wanderer" on an endless quest, and his ceaseless literary activities—figurative wanderings—necessarily fail to find their opposite; although he is "crowned with laurels," he remains "without a home" (81; see 51). Carlyle concludes that Schiller was never able to return home, that he found "no rest, no peace" (203).[3] Had he remained in Würtemberg, he would have been oppressed by an authority that would not permit him to follow a higher calling, but his new-gained literary authority does not permit him to displace the duke so he can return to the childhood idyll.

Instead of creating a promised land into which he could lead his people, Schiller becomes a commercial traveler. Initially, he envisions literature as an idyll that, like the family, exists outside the laws of economy. Before his exile, he claims that he "honour[s]" literature "too highly to wish to live [i.e., make his living] by it," but, when he cuts himself off from "his stepdame home," he must "go forth, though friendless and alone, to seek his fortune in the great *market* of life" that "dissolve[s]" his "connexions" to his family and replaces them with the demands of a multifarious "public" (12, 28, 40; emphasis added). Instead of discovering a new idyll, he works in cities like Leipzig, which is the "centre of . . . commerce of all sorts, that of literature not excepted" (54). Although the bookseller system frees him, as it had others, from dependence on the aristocratic patronage of the duke, he is not truly free, because the new system replaces the law of the patron with the law of the public and its demand for particular kinds of literary commodities. Neither system of production can satisfy Schiller's desire for the transcendental. Although *The Life of Schiller* concludes by affirming the "creed" of literature, it does not successfully envision literature as capable of reproducing the lost idyll.

Carlyle's first major essay on Goethe (1828) solves this problem by separating the loss of home from the act of rebellion and by eliminating the constraints of economy from the representation of the literary career. The essay divides Goethe's life into two phases: that of the youthful "Unbeliever" who wrote *Die Leiden des jungen Werthers*, and that of the mature "Believer" who wrote *Wilhelm Meister* (*CME*, 1:210). Because his father represents the authority of the law, not of religious belief, Goethe's home is not the domestic idyll that Schiller's had been. Goethe's father plays the role that the duke had played in *The Life of Schiller* while the role of Schiller's father is eliminated. Goethe's father represents the law, both because he is a lawyer, and because, like the duke, he commands his son to study the law. Not only does Goethe rebel against the law laid down by his father, but, by refusing to become a lawyer, he questions the authority of his father's career.

Because the religious idyll is absent, Goethe's rebellion is at first only a rejection of his father's authority rather than an attempt to establish his own. Schiller's rebellion against the duke and his adoption of literature had been a single, unified step. The literary career through which he attempted to recuperate the domestic idyll was inextricably linked with the rebellion that made it impossible for him to stop wandering and begin to find his way home. By eliminating the domestic idyll in his narrative of Goethe's career, Carlyle shifted Goethe's rebellion to the first stage of the narrative, separating the rebellious negation from the later affirmation of authority in literature. *The Sorrows of Young Werter* does not yet create a new mythology; it simply negates belief. During his period of "Unbelief," Goethe, like Schiller, becomes a wanderer; blown about by the "Harmattan breath of Doubt," a "nameless Unrest" prevents him from authoring a new idyll (*CME*, 1:216). Only in the second stage of the narrative, when he attains belief, does Goethe become a prophetic author who can lead his people "home" to the promised land (217, 224).

In his essay on Schiller's correspondence (1829; published 1831), Carlyle employs the new structure of "Goethe" to revise the narrative of Schiller's career. Just as he divides Goethe's life into the phases of unbelief and belief, he now divides Schiller's life into the "worldly" epoch before he takes his "Literary Vows" and the "spiritual" epoch afterward (*CME*, 2:175). *The Life of Schiller* had represented both epochs as posing the same problems, his youth divided between the piety of the family and the oppression of the duke, and his literary career divided between his desire for a high calling and the demands of economy. But "Schiller" creates a structural opposition between them: "what lies before this epoch, and what lies after it, have two altogether different characters" (175). Schiller begins life already in the "worldly epoch" of time and history where he experiences the "oppression, distortion, isolation" of economy and the duke's law (177). While the essay mentions a "glad season" of youth at a time when Schiller still lived in the domestic idyll, the two-part structure excludes it from the basic narrative sequence, suggesting that this idyll exists outside of time, in a realm before Schiller's life proper began (178; see *SR*, 90). The piety that had been associated with his family enters the narrative only in the second epoch, when Schiller, now a "priest-like" and "monastic" man of letters, "works and meditates only on what we may call Divine things" (175). The idyll excluded from the beginning of the narrative finally enters it through the activity of the artist. This essay does not, like *The Life of Schiller*, manifest anxiety about the loss of the home in the choice of the literary career, since the family is recuperated in the idyllic community of writers at Weimar, where Schiller triumphs over illness and the demands of economy are eliminated, freeing him to rise "into the highest regions of Art he ever reached" (*CME*, 2:187). In "Schiller," Carlyle goes further than in "Goethe" by representing, even though excluding, the childhood idyll that then becomes the object of the artist's quest and determines that the literary career will take on a more distinctly religious cast. This Schiller not only discovers his authority but fully recovers the realm of the transcendental and discovers a promised land.

Carlyle's Fictions and the Career Narrative

It is appropriate that *Sartor Resartus* portrays an "Editor" patching together Teufelsdröckh's biography from six paper bags of fragments sent from Germany, for Carlyle himself had patched it together from the lives of German authors (see Tennyson, *Sartor*, 87–88, 191, n. 30). Virtually every detail of the biography of Diogenes Teufelsdröckh— himself a German writer—may be found in the sketches of the lives and works of German writers—Musæus, Fouqué, Tieck, Hoffman, Richter, Werner, Heyne, and Novalis as well as Goethe and Schiller— that Carlyle composed between 1823 and 1830. Like the narratives that preceded it, the biography of Teufelsdröckh does not seek to represent Carlyle's life so much as to give it a meaningful shape by constructing a paradigm for the establishment of the literary career.

Carlyle's satirical poem, "Peter Nimmo," and his abandoned novel, "Illudo Chartis," both represent the narrative of loss of authority and religious faith in a comic mode, mocking the world of his youth. "Peter Nimmo" is based on the life of an eccentric scholar who studied for seemingly countless years at the University of Edinburgh. The poem begins with a conversion experience in which Nimmo, "drifting" with no "'fix'd point' . . . thro' some mountain-pass," has a vision and experiences a religious calling, a scene that anticipates, in the mock-spiritual mode, Teufelsdröckh's Everlasting Yea. But the poem treats Nimmo's election with all the skepticism of an Enlightenment critique of enthusiasm. Instead of bringing his wanderings to an end, Nimmo's search for religious truth at the university turns him into an eternal student, an "old wandering Jew" who never completes his studies and never achieves rest. The narrator finally destroys the illusion of Nimmo's divine election by putting out two pints of rum and secretly watching as Nimmo drinks it up and falls down "Dead-drunk." In its treatment of Nimmo's calling, the poem hints at how the university undermined Carlyle's own religious vocation and perhaps attempts to disguise his anxiety by treating the event comically. Written at a time when he had rejected a religious vocation but was still uncertain what vocation might replace it, the poem discovers no faith, no closure, no authority, and no alternative career.[4]

Just as "Peter Nimmo" treats comically the religious calling that Carlyle's parents had sought for him, so "Illudo Chartis," a fragment of a novel that Carlyle began and then quickly abandoned in 1826, parodies Carlyle's family and origins. The fragment has three distinct parts, demarcated by sharp shifts in tone. It begins in a comic mode similar to that of "Peter Nimmo." Like "Nimmo" as well, it does not discover a vocation for the hero, but, unlike "Nimmo," it abandons the comic mode and concludes in the dark mood of *Werter*. In "Peter Nimmo," the skeptical narrator is structurally and dramatically separated from the deluded questor, while the narrator of "Illudo Chartis" treats the hero, Stephen Corry, seriously, displacing the comedy from the hero to the hero's family.

In the first chapter, describing Stephen's origins in the "village of Duckdubs in the south of Scotland," Carlyle comically inverts the characteristics of his own family (King, 164). Corry's parents are of the "lowest sort," his mother a "rampageant quean" and his father an incompetent stonemason whose cottages fall down "before [his] trowel had done pargetting them" (164–65). A mock genealogical investigation discovers that Corry's ancestors were "weak, underfoot, unprosperous . . . all walked with a stoop, all splayed out their feet at a given angle, and all spoke with the same Northumbrian burr" (165–66). The comic details of the narrative—the premature collapse of Corry's cottages and the debilitated male line—manifest the pressure of time on a family that has already fallen into history at the commencement of Stephen Corry's life and is from the beginning exiled from the domestic idyll.

But when the narrative turns to Stephen himself, it changes tone, isolating him from a family corrupted by time and surrounding him with idyllic comforts. It separates him from the family by informing us that he is not like his father and has not inherited any qualities of the debilitated male line. It then situates Duckdubs in a womblike "little circular valley" that anticipates the idyllic Entephul (German for Duckpond) of *Sartor Resartus* (see Cabau, 193–99). By introducing the idyllic mood only after the comic opening, Carlyle displaces it from the aboriginal moment of the narrative just as he had excluded it from the primary narrative structure of "Goethe" and "Schiller."

The idyllic mood is sustained only briefly, however, and when, at the beginning of the second chapter, Stephen's father decides to send him to the University of Edinburgh "in the ever memorable year of 1795," the tone changes again. "To all literary men," the narrator comments, "such an epoch is like a second birth, the cardinal point on which most of their future life revolves" (King, 167). Stephen Corry's history is divided by this "second birth" just as Schiller's and Goethe's lives are divided into two epochs. As previously noted, 1795 was the year in which Carlyle was born and with which he was to end his history of the French Revolution. It is only at this moment that Stephen is exiled from the idyll and enters the temporal realm of his already fallen family. The narrative therefore doubly excludes the idyllic moment by representing 1795, literally the year of Carlyle's birth, as the moment of Stephen's birth into time and consciousness.

The narrative indicts Stephen's father for exiling his son and for allowing the idyll to fall into decay. Rather than being grateful to his father for receiving an education, Stephen leaves his family "sick at heart" and overwhelmed by "a black deep of Discouragement" (168). Attending the university exiles Stephen from home, just as rejecting the law had exiled Schiller and Goethe. But at this point, still a year and a half before he wrote "Goethe," Carlyle could not envision a way to lead Stephen from despair to affirmation and the literary career. Stephen must remain, like the Schiller of the earlier biography, an eternal wanderer.

Carlyle encountered the same problems in the far more ambitious but also unfinished *Wotton Reinfred*, begun in early 1827 soon after he abandoned "Illudo Chartis." It starts where "Illudo Chartis" left off, in the mood of despair, but then attempts to move its hero beyond the moment of despair in order to enable him to return to the idyllic home. By writing first in the mode of *Werter*, then in the mode of *Wilhelm Meister*, Carlyle anticipated the narrative movement from the despair of *Werter* to the belief of *Wilhelm Meister* in "Goethe."[5] But, unlike Goethe and Schiller, who become authors, Wotton remains a passive observer whose career is still undecided when the narrative breaks off.

Wotton Reinfred, like "Illudo Chartis," excludes the childhood idyll by displacing it from the beginning of the narrative. Chapter 1 commences in the mood of despair and unbelief that follows exile from the idyll (the idyll itself does not appear until chapter 2). It associates the idyll with Reinfred's mother, whose soul is "full of loftiest religion," while his father, a "man of an equal but stern and indignant temper" is associated with the wrathful god who exiles sinners from the maternal paradise (14–15, 13). The death of his father when Wotton is still in "early boyhood" suggests that, since the father creates and sustains the idyll, it disappears with his death, which therefore constitutes exile (13).[6] On the advice of the male authorities who replace his father (his pastor and teacher), Wotton is sent, like Stephen Corry, from home to the university, where the study of logic, mathematics, and science, as well as French philosophy, lead him to the "utter negation" and "doubt" with which the narrative begins (24, 22). The encircling walls of the home (which recall the "circular valley" of "Illudo Chartis") are replaced by the "prison" walls that close him out of the childhood paradise (36).

The remainder of the narrative represents Wotton's quest to escape this prison and recover the childhood idyll. Yet he does not try to obtain the authority of the father who created the idyll, and the narrative persistently suggests that his rediscovered idylls are illusions. He first hopes to recover the idyll through love. When he meets Jane Montagu, the "black walls of his prison" melt away, revealing a new "garden of Eden," but this "celestial vision" quickly gives way to a "grim world" of Werterian despair when Jane's relatives forbid her to see Wotton and arrange her engagement to Edmund Walter, a "man of rank" (36, 39, 38). It is at this chronological moment that the narrative of *Wotton Reinfred* begins, Wotton's friend Bernard suggesting that in order to resolve his troubles he undertake a journey, the curative journey of novels like *Wilhelm Meister* in which the experience of the journey enables the questing hero to return to the idyllic home. But, unlike Meister's, Reinfred's "travels" last for only one brief chapter, at which point he discovers a new idyll or "Elysium," the House of the Wold (55). His sojourn at the House of the Wold, during which he joins in lengthy discussions of transcendental philosophy, occupies about a third of the text; yet at the conclusion of these discussions, Wotton has not gained the authority to create his own idyll. Because he discovers the House accidentally, not through the rigors of the quest, he does not become a member of this ideal society.[7] Appropriately, he is driven from the idyll by the unexpected appearance of Edmund Walter, the rival who had deprived him of his previous idyll, Jane Montagu.

The narrative concludes with Jane Montagu's own story—Wotton has encountered her while fleeing from the House of the Wold—which reinforces the pattern of recovery and exile from the idyll. Although Jane's narrative is based roughly on the life of Mme. de Staël's Corinne, to whom Jane compares herself, it almost exactly repeats the narrative of Wotton's life. Like Wotton, Jane has lost her father early in life and become "an orphan wanderer," exiled from an idyllic childhood (130; see 134–35). Yet in the career of Jane Montagu, Carlyle introduces what is missing in the life of Wotton Reinfred. Jane longs, like Corinne, to be a poet, hoping that through this means she can gain independence from the interdicting family and the ability to create her own domestic idyll. But her quest, too, remains incomplete, because the strictures society places on women prevent her from achieving authority. By explaining that it was not her desire to reject Wotton— she is just as much the victim of Edmund Walter and the interdicting family as he—and by suggesting a complementarity between her desire to be a poet and Wotton's freedom to be one, Jane's story offers the possibility of a reconciliation that would resolve the dramatic problem with which the narrative begins (that is, their separation) and so constitute a domestic idyll. But the resolution toward which the narrative appears to be moving does not provide the means for transferring poetic authority to Wotton. The manuscript breaks off at the point where Jane concludes her narrative, and neither Jane nor Wotton is any closer to completing the quest.

The biography of Diogenes Teufelsdröckh in *Sartor Resartus* attempts to solve the problems of the earlier fictions by borrowing structural elements from the biographies. Its explicit narrative structure is the two-part structure of the 1827–28 essays on Goethe and Schiller, the movement from unbelief to belief that excludes an initial moment of idyllic belief and implies an imminent three-part structure of belief/unbelief/recovered belief. In these essays, this structural sequence is elaborated through the search for the career and the topos of the journey. The sequence of careers—the religious ministry, the law, and literature as substitute for religion—corresponds to the movement from belief to unbelief to recovery of belief. The journey motif translates this sequence into the sequence of exile from the domestic idyll, desert wanderings, and the return home. Just as the explicit two-part structure excludes the initial moment of belief in the case of Goethe, so it excludes the primal home and the religious career.

The biography of Teufelsdröckh employs the same structure. Teufelsdröckh is banished from the "Idyll" of Entephul, descends to the nadir of the Everlasting No, and finally achieves the celestial heights of the Everlasting Yea. The primal idyll is excluded in several ways. First, the narrator informs us, in the chapter entitled "Genesis," that Teufels-dröckh was born not in Entephul but in the transcendental realm, "so that this Genesis of his can properly be nothing but an Exodus" (81). From birth, he begins wandering in the desert. Second, unlike Schiller, Richter, Heyne, Musæus, Peter Nimmo, and Carlyle himself, but like Goethe, Teufelsdröckh does not begin life with the intention of pursuing a religious career; he pursues only the two vocations of law and authorhood. At the same time that *Sartor Resartus* excludes the religious vocation, however, it introduces the element missing from the earlier fictions, the possibility of a literary vocation. Finally, the Editor, in patching together the biography from the six bags of auto-biographical fragments, inserts the idyllic moment at the beginning of the narrative; but the first fragment quoted by the Editor comes from a bag marked with the zodiacal sign of Libra that, corresponding to the beginning of autumn, hardly seems appropriate for the beginning of life and a paradisal idyll.

The chapter entitled "Idyllic" goes out of its way to emphasize that Teufelsdröckh has been excluded from the idyll from the be-ginning. Initially, Entephul (Duckpond), where his family occupies a "Cottage, embowered in fruit-trees and forest-trees, evergreens and honeysuckles," does seem idyllic (83). Teufelsdröckh's honest parents resemble the good parents of Richter, Goethe, Burns, Heyne, Schiller, and Novalis.[8] The chapter commences by attributing the "Happy sea-son of Childhood" to "Kind Nature, that art to all a bountiful mother," and the transcendental plenitude of this natural world is represented by the piety of his foster mother who, like Wotton's and Novalis's mothers, teaches him "her own simple version of the Christian Faith" (90, 99).

But, as in the earlier narratives, the possibility of exile from the maternal idyll exists from the beginning in the figure of the father.[9] Whereas Teufelsdröckh's mother is "in the strictest acceptation Reli-gious," his father attends church only as a "parade-duty" (99). The explicit contrast, which suggests that Andreas is not genuinely reli-gious, associates him with the law rather than belief. While the mother is so closely identified with the idyll—she is mother nature—that she is indistinguishable from it, the father has created the idyll and is thus separate from it as the creator is separate from the creation. At the same time, the father lives in his own creation and, as its author and authority, possesses the power to exclude his children from it. Whereas the mother imbues the idyll with a sense of unity, the father, who shares the "rugged[ness]" of Goethe's father and the sternness of Wotton Reinfred's, lays down the law and alienates the son from it (*WM*, 1:13). The "paternal Cottage" that protects the idyll also "shuts us in" and compels Teufelsdröckh to "Obedience" (*SR*, 90). Consequently, just as Schiller encounters the constraints of the duke, so Teufelsdröckh's "Active Power" is "hemmed in" and the timeless idyll becomes a prison (98).

Fathers and father substitutes exile Schiller, Stephen Corry, Wotton Reinfred, and Diogenes Teufelsdröckh from the domestic idyll by sending them to school. In *Sartor Resartus*, the father's authority becomes the authoritarian discipline of the Hinterschlag (Strike-behind) Gymnasium. The father exiles the child not only by removing him from the idyllic home but also by inserting him into a temporal, urban world of unbelief. Significantly, the first objects that Teufelsdröckh encounters as he enters town on his way to school are the town's steeple-clock and jail, signs of his entry into the prison of finitude. The rural idyll becomes urban prison; the father as creator and sustainer of the idyll becomes oppressor who exiles the child from Eden.

As in *Wotton Reinfred*, Carlyle represents the loss of the idyll as the loss of its creator and sustainer, a loss emphasized in *Sartor Resartus* by repetition. The first instance is Teufelsdröckh's separation from his "real" father in heaven (Andreas Futteral is only a stepfather) which is coterminous with his entry into life and time. Teufelsdröckh expresses a longing to know this "unknown Father's name," but discovers that he is unknowable and therefore unable to sustain Teufelsdröckh's transcendental existence (86). (The special role of the father is suggested as well by Teufelsdröckh's total lack of interest in his unknown mother.) The unknown father exiles and orphans him in the temporal world just as Andreas will exile him by sending him to school, leaving him "orphaned and alone." Teufelsdröckh's second loss is the death of Andreas, which occurs when he is only twelve, another instance in which Teufelsdröckh's life parallels Wotton Reinfred's.[10] Because Teufelsdröckh learns simultaneously that Andreas has died and that Andreas is not his real father, he now feels "doubly orphaned" (107). The symbolic import of Carlyle's use of the orphan theme here is given special emphasis by the fact that this event is distinctly nonautobiographical. Carlyle did not lose his father as a child; indeed, his father was still alive when, at the age of thirty-five, he wrote *Sartor Resartus*, the last of a series of "autobiographical" narratives in which the father dies. The death of the father represents the loss of the idyll, since the father creates and sustains it, but it also represents exile from Eden as punishment of the rebellious son who desires to possess the idyll for himself. In this respect, the narrative imaginatively kills off the father in order to enable the son to replace him. Since killing off the figure of authority has the immediate consequence of destroying the authority that sustains the idyll, which must then be restored and recreated, *Sartor Resartus* opens up the possibility that a rebellious son can become an authority, an author.

By exiling his son from the transcendental realm and sending him to a "Rational University," the father also deprives him of religious belief. Just as Adam and Eve are exiled from the garden because they desire knowledge, Teufelsdröckh is exiled from the world of his father by the education that undermines his religious faith. At the university, Teufelsdröckh, like Goethe, feels the "Harmattan-wind" or "fever-paroxysms of Doubt" and falls under the spell of "the nightmare, Unbelief" (*SR*, 186, 114; *CME*, 1:216). Their education substitutes authoritarian law, which divides everything into right and wrong, good and evil, for unified belief. The legal career comes to represent for Teufelsdröckh, as it does for Schiller and Goethe, imprisonment by the laws of rational economy.

Believing, like Schiller, that he is destined for a "high[er] vocation," Teufelsdröckh "breaks off his neck-halter" (Richter also "broke loose" from his first vocation to become a literary man) and rejects the legal profession (*SR*, 119, 121; *CME*, 2:114). But, unlike Schiller, he does not immediately take up the literary profession because, in the process of freeing him from the imprisoning structures of the law of the father, his rebellion destroys those structures and leaves him without any form of belief. At this point, he resembles instead the Goethe of *Werter*, who has not yet achieved the "high calling" of literature. Teufelsdröckh's search for knowledge continues the enlightenment project against which it rebels. His wanderings begin when he walks to school, intensify when he escapes the law and begins searching for a place in society, and reach their height after he is rejected by Blumine. Not only does his rebellion divide him from the still center of the domestic idyll, it thrusts him into a life of restless, apparently endless, wandering.

Because knowledge is never certain, the search for it can never end. Teufelsdröckh needs knowledge to obtain authority, but he can only achieve authority and rest when he stops seeking knowledge. In the prelapsarian idyll, where belief is stable, everything is known and the search for knowledge is unnecessary as well as unthinkable—the mind is unaware of itself. In the search for knowledge, the mind becomes aware of itself and the limits of its knowledge; it becomes self-conscious. Carlyle borrowed Novalis's philosophy of *entsagen*—the renunciation of self-consciousness—to solve Teufelsdröckh's dilemma.[11] Like Teufelsdröckh, Novalis discovers this philosophy after the loss of his youthful love, Sophie (*CME*, 2:12–17). Only after Novalis and Teufelsdröckh attain a new belief by adopting the philosophy of renunciation do they become authors. The son's self-negation gives him the authority to restore his lost father to the world; Teufelsdröckh discovers that nature is not a dead machine but "godlike and my Father's" (*SR*, 188). Teufelsdröckh's discovery of his vocation as author of a "new Mythus" completes the unfinished narratives of Carlyle's previous fictions—Peter Nimmo, Stephen Corry, and Wotton Reinfred do not discover any profession—and places him in the company of Goethe and Schiller (194).

Authoring the Author

At the same time he was formulating the history of the loss and recuperation of authority in his biographies of German writers and fictional characters, Carlyle was representing his own history in his letters and journals. Although his loss of faith and abandonment of a religious calling appears to have been a gradual process, he represented it in later years as a cataclysmic event resulting from his reading of Gibbon: "I read Gibbon, and then first clearly saw that Christianity was not true" (Allingham, *Diary*, 232).[12] The authority of miracles—a form of revelation, as they manifest the divine in the realm of the human—had been at the forefront of the debate on revelation since the seventeenth century. Carlyle describes Gibbon's attack on "the orthodox belief in miracles" as the central event in his loss of faith. His first reading of the *Decline and Fall* in its entirety—between November 1817 and February 1818—is almost certainly combined in his representations of the event with his decision, just a few months earlier, to abandon his studies for the ministry (*CL*, 1:112, 115). Six months before he read

Gibbon, he had announced to his friend Robert Mitchell that "every 'true religion' is propped & bolstered, & the hand of its rivals tied up; till by nursing and fattening it has become a bloated monster that human nature can no longer look upon—and men rise up & knock its brains out" (*CL*, 1:99). When assessing the importance of Gibbon to this process, it is important to keep in mind that Carlyle had already decided that the religious vocation was no longer a high one, it too having been reduced to a "trade" (*CL*, 1:60). Carlyle did not just accidently turn to Gibbon at this moment; he was seeking in his history the means to knock the brains out of a bloated Christianity.

Although the idea of earning his living as a writer occurred early— in 1814 he envisioned himself as attaining "literary fame," and in 1817 he began his first attempts at professional writing—literature did not initially represent for Carlyle a means of achieving authority, replacing the religious vocation, and recovering the domestic idyll (Kaplan, 39). From 1817 into the mid-1820s, he contemplated several careers, only slowly establishing himself as a professional writer. After rejecting schoolteaching and pursuing studies in mathematics and science that might lead to a university career, he enrolled, in 1819, as a law student. This brief episode later enabled him to identify with Goethe and Schiller, although it is important to note that in Carlyle's case it was not the law but the religious vocation that had been imposed by paternal authority. *Sartor Resartus*, in representing Teufelsdröckh constrained by the law rather than religion, disguises the fact that Carlyle had rebelled against the very religious authority that he sought to recuperate.

It was not until Carlyle encountered the German Romantics that he began to represent literature as a replacement for religion.[13] He began learning German in 1819, and by the middle of 1820 was writing that German literature promised to reveal a "new Heaven and new Earth" (*CL*, 1:268). He learned from the Germans to represent literature as the new liturgy: from Goethe's Wilhelm Meister, who tells his friend Werner that "it was the poet . . . that first formed gods for us; that exalted us to them, and brought them down to us" (*WM*, 1:114); from Schiller, whom he depicted as an "Apostle" whose "creed" was "Literature" (*LS*, 200); and from Fichte's *On the Nature of the Literary Man*, which depicts authors as the "appointed interpreters" of the "Divine Idea," a "perpetual priesthood . . . standing forth . . . as the dispensers and living types of God's everlasting wisdom" (*CME*,

1:58). This myth of poetic inspiration and genius represented poets as transhistorical individuals whose visionary capacity gives them the transcendental authority of both prophets and kings. Since literary men were prophets who would constitute the new church, their literary productions would be its liturgy and revealed texts, replacing the discourse of Christianity with literary discourse. Carlyle consistently depicted the writers he most admired, especially Goethe, as priests and prophets, and German literature became his Bible (*CL*, 6:271, 7:3; *SR*, 252–53).[14] The literary artist reinstitutes revelation, Fichte's literary man, for example, manifesting a "Divine Idea." "Every man that writes," he concluded, "is writing a new Bible; or a new Apochrypha; to last for a week, or for a thousand years" (*TNB*, 264). By the time he wrote his essay on Burns in 1828, he could claim that "Poetry . . . is but another form of Wisdom, of Religion," and, by the 1830s, the notion that "Literature is fast becoming . . . [a] Church" in which the man of letters is "Pope" had become a commonplace in his writings (*CME*, 1:314, 2:369–70; see 3:201–2; *TNB*, 223).[15]

Because literature recuperates theocracy, the author is not only prophet but king, producing the texts of the law as well as of belief (*CME*, 2:370). Just as literary authors create new beliefs and new Bibles, they also create new laws as "legislators" and lawmakers.[16] Goethe is "king of himself and of his world," superior to Napoleon and Charles XII, and Burns, a "Napoleon among the crowned sovereigns of modern Politics" (*WM*, 1:24; *CME*, 1:297).[17] A journal entry made in early 1831 envisions in the poet the theocratic union of prophet and king that supplants feudal monarchy: since King William—the heir to feudal monarchy—has become a "usurper," the "only Sovereigns of the world in these days are the Literary men (were there any such in Britain), the Prophets. It is always a Theocracy; the King has to be anointed by the Priest, and now the Priest (Goethe for example) will not . . . consecrate the existing King, who therefore is a usurper, and reigns only by sufferance" (*TNB*, 184).

In 1822, Carlyle's first article on German literature appeared, and his career as translator and promoter of German literature, a career that would continue until 1832, had begun. By early 1825, he had adopted as his "very creed" the passage—translated and quoted at length in his *Life of Schiller*—in which Schiller condemned hack writing and depicted literature as a high vocation, making its aim "philosophy, religion, art" (*CL*, 3:271; *LS*, 200; see 201–2). Although still a hack writer, Carlyle had raised himself to the level of the translator and interpreter of the new prophets, enabling him to claim to his mother that he was after all "a kind of missionary" (*CL*, 4:180).

The adoption of this creed—the creed that men of letters could create a new creed—was crucial to the recovery of belief Carlyle achieved during the famous Leith Walk episode in 1822. In retrospect, this episode, like his reading of Gibbon, acquired special importance for Carlyle, so much so that he claimed late in life that the Rue St. Thomas de l'Enfer episode of *Sartor Resartus* "occurred quite literally to myself in Lieth [*sic*] Walk" (*TR*, 49). But this event, which passed unnoticed in his letters and even in the privacy of his journal, only became significant in retrospect when combined with the discovery of the Germans (see Moore, "Carlyle's Conversion"). A new realm of possibilities had opened up in that year when he published his first essay on German literature ("Faustus") and began making the transition from student of German literature to preacher of its doctrines. Although still without his own authority, he was no longer hacking at encyclopedia articles and translations of geometry, but proclaiming a new gospel. His claim that he was "indebted to *Goethe*" for the Leith Walk experience suggests that what actually happened in 1822 was that he began to envision the achievement of authority through literature (*Rem.*, 282).

By 1827, Carlyle had formulated the narrative of a career in which literature recuperates lost religious faith, enabling one to return home by recreating the lost domestic idyll. This "history" is outlined in one of his earliest letters to Goethe:

> I was once an Unbeliever . . . exasperated, wretched, driven almost to despair; so that Faust's wild *curse* seemed the only fit greeting for human life. . . . But now, thank Heaven, all this is altered . . . I look forward with cheefulness to a life spent in Literature. . . . No wonder I should love the wise and worthy men by whose instructions so blessed a result has been brought about! For these men too there can be no reward like that consciousness that . . . those that are wandering in darkness turn towards them as to . . . loadstars guiding into a secure home. (*CL*, 4:248)

In discovering his authority and creating a "period of new Spirituality and Belief, in the midst of old Doubt and Denial . . . wherein Reverence is again rendered compatible with Knowledge, and Art and Religion are one," Goethe had enabled Carlyle to establish his own authority as well (*CL*, 5:106).[18]

Because Carlyle's authority could not take the form of the religious authority of the pious father who had never experienced doubt, he had to imagine his own authority, his ability to become a father, via the model of Goethe. In June 1824, Carlyle wrote Goethe of his need to "pour out before [him], as before a *father*, the woes and wanderings of a heart whose mysteries you seemed so thoroughly to comprehend" (*CL*, 3:87; emphasis added).[19] From this time forward, Carlyle adopted Goethe as his "spiritual Father" (*CL*, 4:209; see 248, 408). The authority lost with the death of the father must be recovered in a new father figure. Just as Teufelsdröckh discovers his authority in the moment that he rediscovers the presence of his father in the universe, so Carlyle's adoption of Goethe as father signified the recovery of authority that validated his literary career.

Yet if Carlyle was to be an authority in his own right, he could not be content to proclaim the gospel of German literature; he must produce his own sacred texts. So long as he could only preach the gospel of German literature and was unable to preach his own, his calling remained an "Egyptian bondage" (*CL*, 4:102; see 1:310, 2:145–46, 3:4, 10, 23, 5:226, 230, 214, 285–86, 303). Despite protestations that "literature is the *wine* of life; it will not, cannot, be its *food*," he had to find his food, and later Jane's as well, through writing (*CL*, 3:244; see 5:237). But he insisted that literature, which was "another name for . . . Religion," could be distinguished from "Periodical writing" (*CL*, 5:250–51; see 254–55; *TNB*, 170–71). As early as 1821, he declared that he wanted to "*write a book* for [his] own convenience," a longing that persisted in his subsequent desire to create "a *Kunstwerk* of [his] own" (*CL*, 1:399, 3:407). Yet, before 1830, he managed only three unsuccessful attempts to write a novel.[20] Although he could represent others recovering authority, he could not recover authority himself until he created his own authoritative text. *Sartor Resartus* was especially important as an attempt to break out of the bounds of political economy. With it, Carlyle not only enacted the mythology of the literary career by producing a narrative in which the hero becomes an author, he also succeeded in creating his first original work of literature. In addition to representing the recuperation of authority in the career of Teufelsdröckh, Carlyle hoped this work would establish his own authority as a man of letters.

Crisis in the Career: "The Reminiscence of James Carlyle"

The representation of Teufelsdröckh's achievement of authority did not attain transcendental authority for Carlyle. As we shall see in the following chapter, the authority achieved in *Sartor Resartus* remains problematic. But even putting that aside, the book could not establish Carlyle's authority when he completed it in 1831 because he could not get it published, the publishers rejecting, in effect, his authority. Six months after taking the manuscript to London to seek a publisher, he still remained there, but he had given up hope of getting *Sartor* into print. At this point his father died, and he expressed his anxieties about his tenuous authority in the "Reminiscence of James Carlyle." Although Thomas Carlyle the narrator attempts to revive and assume the authority of his father by literally authoring him in the memoir and making him the model of his own authority, the themes of loss, exile, and death insistently suggest the radical distance between father and son, and so the impossibility of achieving authority.

In "The Reminiscence of James Carlyle," as in the previous narratives, the future author's family resides in a theocratic idyll. Whereas his predecessors represented the dominance of the law over belief, James Carlyle represents the ideal union of belief and the law. His belief is authoritative, both in the sense that it is unshakeable—he is "never visited with Doubt"—and in the sense that it enables him to author or create a religious ethos for his family that he introduces into the Burgher Seceder sect (4; see 9–10). He also participates in and affirms the hierarchical order through which the transcendental authority of religion is transmitted into the polity. Within the family, James Carlyle is the head, a natural aristocrat and communal patriarch who pays his men "*handsomely* and with overplus," and he in turn defers to the Scottish gentry because they are the "true 'ruler[s]' of the people'" (11, 8). These hierarchical gradations of authority ordain and sustain a stable and just social order. The Carlyles are ideally situated between the corrupting wealth of aristocracy and the severe poverty that strikes many of their neighbors during the "dear years" of

1799–1800. As in Gaskell's representation of the pastoral family, the domestic economy of the Carlyles promotes a community of interests uncontaminated by the individualism of political economy.

James Carlyle's authority as leader of the religious community, respectable citizen, and father is embodied in his skill as a mason, a craft he practiced from the age of fifteen to the age of fifty-seven, some seven years after Carlyle left home for the university. James Carlyle built the house in which his family lived, symbolically constructing the structure of belief through which they lived their lives. His buildings function, like the Bible, as sources of authority, of belief and law; they are sacred "texts . . . of the Gospel of man's Free-will" (2).[21]

Although James Carlyle's buildings function like sacred writings, the fact that they are made of stone distinguishes them from paper documents—most certainly from the writings of his son. Like sacred texts, James Carlyle's buildings incorporate the transcendental into the material; his labors lay the "foundations" of a heavenly "city" (31). Carlyle emphasizes this process in his discussion of the first project his father worked on, the bridge at Auld Garth. In *Sartor Resartus*, the "Bridge-builder" is a "Pontifex, or Pontiff," the "Poet and inspired Maker" of symbols that combine the natural and the supernatural (79, 225). Carlyle draws on the etymological derivation and the historical application of the term *pontiff* to suggest that the bridge-builder is a religious authority who builds bridges between the realms of everyday life and the supernatural.[22] Consequently, Auld Garth bridge, as Carlyle represents it, partakes of the transcendental, remaining unchanged in the fifty years since it was built even though all around it has altered: "The Auldgarth Bridge still spans the water, silently defies its chafing . . . O Time! O Time! wondrous and fearful art thou; yet there is in man what is above thee" (24).

Thus Carlyle makes the very substantiality of masonry—James Carlyle becomes a mason in an era of "Substance and Solidity"—the emblem of his father's ability to bridge the gulf between the natural and the supernatural (5, 23; see 31). By filling the natural world, a world that consists only of insubstantial "husks" of things, with the reality of divine presence, he gives substance and solidity to that world, a plenitude that manifests itself in the fertility of the pastoral idyll (5; see 28). Work—James Carlyle's "great maxim" is "That man was created to work"—becomes the human equivalent of divine creation (5). In equating his father's power and authority with that of kings, Carlyle emphasizes this procreative capacity: James Carlyle is "a true Workman in this vineyard of the Highest: be his work that of Palace-building and Kingdom-founding, or only of delving and ditching, to me it is no matter" (3). The king and the mason are united in the Palace-builder, a man who creates the building that houses the royal family, but also a father who builds the hereditary dynasty. Furthermore, Carlyle equates the creation of a human society—a king founding a land or nation—with the substantial act of ditching and delving that makes land arable. Not surprisingly, when the "industrious" James Carlyle turns from masoncraft to farming, he remains equally creative: "Two ears of corn are now in many places growing where he found only one" (24, 31). Not only does this activity make the land produce, it is irreversible, leaving a permanent mark: "a portion of this Planet bears beneficent traces of his strong Hand and strong Head" (2). The text of James Carlyle's teaching here takes its most substantial form, and this image of turning wasteland into productive tillage would become a major topos in Carlyle's later writings.

Carlyle's narrative does not so much recover James Carlyle's world in the process of representing it as mourn its passing. The form of the narrative radically separates the narrating son from the narrated father, who exist in parallel narratives, the narrative in which Carlyle writes—referring to London and the present—and the narrative in which his father lives—referring to Ecclefechan and the past. Carlyle wrote the reminiscence at intervals over the four-day period from Wednesday evening, January 25, 1832—the day after he learned of his father's death—to Sunday evening, January 29—two days after the funeral. He records the individual times of writing (Wednesday evening, Thursday morning and evening, Friday during the funeral and in the evening, and Saturday evening) in the text of the reminiscence and comments on events in the present like the funeral and the condolatory visit of the Irvings. These references to the act of writing frame the reminiscence, separating the rememberer from the remembered. While the form of the private memoir and the tone of loss suggest an emotional union with his father, the fact that the intention to write it appears to have been premeditated suggests a more ritualistic distance. When Teufelsdröckh's father dies, Diogenes writes a "Character" in which, like Carlyle, he speaks of his father's "natural ability" and "deserts in life" and makes "long historical inquiries into the genealogy of the . . . Family" (107). The death of the "real" James Carlyle becomes submerged in the symbolic death of the father already imagined in "Illudo Chartis," *Wotton Reinfred*, and *Sartor Resartus*. Although, in the conclusion of his narrative, Teufelsdröckh appears to recover the lost authority of his father, Carlyle finds that in January 1832 he can only reenact the moment of loss.

While representing James Carlyle as the creator of eternal structures, both domestic and institutional, the reminiscence repeatedly mourns the passing of the world he created. Although that world is timeless and so not subject to decay, the narrator resides in a historical realm, radically cut off from the timeless idyll that exists only in relation to his father. "With him," Carlyle writes, "a whole three-score-and-ten years of the Past has doubly died for me" (33). Carlyle intimates that this loss predates the literal death of the father when he tells us that his earliest recollection—experienced when he was only two years old—is of the "united pangs of Loss and of Remorse" (29). Although he depicts his father living in a timeless idyll, Carlyle describes his own experience as a series of losses, the death not only of his father, but of two uncles, a grandfather, and his sister Margaret. Like the "doubly orphaned" Teufelsdröckh, Carlyle feels that his father is "doubly" dead.

The reminiscence persistently emphasizes the distance between father and son. The idyll dies with the death of its creator and sustainer, James Carlyle, who lived in "the ruins of a falling Era," and consequently has not "left his fellow" (13, 7). After his death, the religious faith that is the foundation of the domestic idyll becomes inaccessible. He belongs to the "*second* race of religious men in Annandale," but "there is no third rising" (26). Carlyle implies that he should have belonged to that latter generation just as, when he underscores the word "he" in the sentence "*He* was never visited with Doubt," he implies that others, including himself, do doubt; as he writes elsewhere: "I cannot remember that I, at that age, had any such force of belief" (19). Just as there is no new religious generation, his father's respect for the political hierarchy is "perhaps no longer possible," and just as he contrasts his own doubt with his father's faith, he recalls his own rebellion against the gentry and social hierarchy when he writes that his father "was there to be governed" and therefore "did not *revolt*" (31). In the absence of the theocratic combination of religious and political authority, political economy emerges to ruin masoncraft by substituting "*show* and *cheapness*" for "Substance" (31).

Even in Carlyle's own special realm of activity, language, James Carlyle possesses a creative power to make transcendental meaning that is no longer available to his son. Since Carlyle shares the traditional suspicion that tropes substitute persuasive expression for real meaning, he contrasts his father's "clear" language of "full *white* sunlight" to the obscuring "*colours*" of rhetoric. James Carlyle's "potent words" make us see the things he speaks of, his "bold glowing style," both "energetic" and "emphatic," "render[ing] visible" his meaning (3–4). He talks as much as the average man, Carlyle concludes, but "by extent of meaning communicated" he says far more because he never uses words for their own sake, always subordinating them to the concrete effects they are intended to produce (6). He is "a man of Action, even with Speech subservient thereto"; like "sharp arrows," his words rend "asunder [the] official sophistries" of the law, enabling him to produce "natural justice" (9, 4, 6).

In this portrait, Carlyle privileges speech over writing, thus differentiating his father's use of language from his own. James Carlyle's language produces the same plenitude as his masonry, while Thomas's words are as ephemeral as the paper on which they are written. Whereas Carlyle has chosen writing as his vocation, his father exhibits his character most fully by "silence" in the midst of dispute (32). Even when he does speak, his words partake more of silence than of speech, since they efface themselves before the truths they represent or the actions they effect; they are articulated silences that give direct access to the transcendental signified. While James Carlyle can complete his silent substantial work and "rest from [his] labours" in the idyll he has created, his son's highly self-referential writings, which draw attention to the surface of writing itself, open up an endless discourse that constantly attempts, but fails, to author the lost idyll (2). Carlyle can only conclude his description of his father's language by lamenting its inaccessibility: "Never shall we again hear such speech as that was . . . *Ach, und dies alles ist hin* [Ah, and this is all gone forever]!" (3–4).

Carlyle, however, blames his father, not just himself, for the loss of the maternal idyll. Early in the reminiscence, Carlyle insists that it had been his father "*exclusively* that determined on *educating* me . . . and made me whatever I am or may become" (2–3). Like his predecessors, James Carlyle exiles his son from the domestic idyll by forcing on him an urban education, an act that entails his separation from "Mother" and "Home" (29–30).[23] That Carlyle associates the world from which he is exiled with home and mother rather than with his father indicates the extent to which the father is not what Carlyle longs for or misses in his exile. The father is simply the possessor of the idyll who has the power to exile his son from it. The loss of the mother manifests itself by her almost total exclusion from the reminiscence, a variant of the excluded idyll in Carlyle's earlier narratives. Carlyle was deeply attached to his mother, as his loving letters demonstrate, yet he excluded her not only from the "Reminiscence of James Carlyle" but from *The Reminiscences* as a whole; he mentions her only briefly, representing her, like the mothers of his German heroes and his fictional characters, as a religious woman descended of "the pious, the just and wise" (27).[24] The mother as idyll cannot be represented or recovered; she can only be mourned for, her absence indicated. Consequently, the reminiscence cannot return him to his mother or her domestic idyll; it can only attempt to cover over the loss of them.[25]

When he exiles his son to the urban academy, the father transforms the protective walls of the home into the oppressive walls of the prison. Excluded from the realm of his mother's belief, the son experiences the law laid down by his father as an "inflexible . . . Authority encircl[ing]" the family (28). While this circle, like the house he built for his family, protects, it also encloses and confines, and Carlyle portrays his father as a man enclosed within the encircling walls he has constructed for himself. As opposed to his much-travelled son, he is "limited to a circle of some forty miles diameter," a circle that becomes a barrier "wall[ing] in . . . [h]is heart" so that his family, even his wife, cannot "freely love him." The circle finally contracts to a point, the narrow world of a man who, though "genuine and coherent, 'living and life-giving,'" remains but "half developed" (10). The James Carlyle of the reminiscence is an arbiter of the law concerned with the most trivial transgressions, even his friends' card playing and his own father's fondness for reading fiction. From this point of view, he is not so much God the loving progenitor as the "dreaded" God of "wrath," an "irascible, choleric" man who creates "an atmosphere of Fear" and "awe" rather than love and protection; "To me," Carlyle concludes, "it was especially so" (6, 10, 28).

Bound within the narrow confines of the law, Carlyle can only establish his authority by rebelling against his father and breaking down the walls of his prison. The "Reminiscence of James Carlyle" suggests the possibility that he might obtain his father's authority by imitating it. Carlyle insists throughout that he must "imitate" his father, admonishing himself to "write my books as he built his Houses" and to become a "continuation, and *second volume* of my Father" (2, 7, 33; see 3, 4, 7, 10, 19–20, 33–34; *CL*, 6:109, 111). But, when the father becomes the law that deprives the son of belief, the son can no longer discover authority, authority that unites law and belief, by imitating the father. He can only discover it by rebelling against the law of the father. Revolution is both an exterior force that intrudes on the domestic idyll, forcing history upon it, and an inner force that enables the prisoner to break out of the prison, to break down the walls of the finite in order to reattain the transcendental: "The great world-revolutions send in their disturbing billows to the remotest creek; and the overthrow of thrones more slowly overturns also the households of the lowly" (30). Just as the revolutionaries in France had torn down the Bastille, so the son tears down the walls of his prison in the hope of building a new home.

Carlyle's rebellion asserts his own authority, his ability to write books as his father built houses, but it also inserts him into the circuit of desire that constantly undermines authority. In *Sartor Resartus*, he had claimed superiority to his father by arguing that books are far more lasting than bridges, that the author of a book has "built what will outlast all marble and metal, and be . . . a Temple, and Seminary and Prophetic Mount" (173). But in the "Reminiscence of James Carlyle" he reverses himself, asserting that "a good Building will last longer than most Books, than one Book of a million" (24). If the "Reminiscence of James Carlyle" suggests the son's need to rebel, it also manifests the son's anxiety that his rebellion will not lead to the establishment of renewed authority, that *Sartor Resartus* had not created a new home or a new "Mythus" but only reenforced the walls of his prison.

THREE

Revolution and Authority:
1830–1837

WHEN CARLYLE BEGAN authoring his own works in the 1830s, he made the search for authority in an era of revolution his major theme. His first attempt to resolve the problem, *Sartor Resartus*, led to the crisis of authority displayed in "The Reminiscence of James Carlyle." In reaction, he reformulated his poetics and produced a work that directly addressed the problem of authority in an era of revolution, *The French Revolution*. But this masterpiece in turn opened up a new realm of revolutionary discourse, leading him to the conclusion that writing alone would never recover the domestic idyll.

Sartor Resartus and the Revolution of 1830

Carlyle watched with interest when, on July 27, 1830, a second French revolution overturned the Bourbon monarchy.[1] In England, parliamentary elections earlier the same month had begun to raise the issues that led to the passage of the Reform Bill in 1832. Throughout the month of August, almost certainly inspired by his reflections on the *sansculottes*—"men without trousers"—Carlyle began to develop in his letters and notebooks the clothing metaphor of *Sartor Resartus*.[2] On August 6, less than two weeks after the revolution began, he was advising his brother that "Men are but poor spindle-shanked wiffling *wonners* [wonders] when you clutch them thro' the mass of *drapery* they wear" (*CL*, 5:130; see 133). By September, he had begun writing the first draft of *Sartor Resartus*, "Thoughts on Clothes" (see *TNB*, 176, 177).[3]

Carlyle completed the long essay that was eventually to become *Sartor Resartus* on October 28, just two weeks before Wellington re-

signed as prime minister, making way for a Whig ministry and par-
liamentary reform. The July elections had returned the Tories, but
Wellington could not suppress the demand for reform in Parliament.
The events in France convinced many that reform was the only alter-
native to revolution. When Grey succeeded Wellington that autumn,
Carlyle shared the general expectation that radical change was immi-
nent: "The Whigs in office, and Baron Brougham Lord Chancellor!
Hay-stacks and corn-stacks burning over all the South and Middle of
England! Where will it end? Revolution on the back of Revolution for
a century yet?" (*TNB*, 178–79).

If Carlyle had reservations about Whig reform, it was because it did
not go far enough, not because, as the Tories argued, it was too revolutionary (Briggs, 237). Carlyle, who considered that the Whigs, like the
Tories, were already "done" for, agreed with the radicals that England
required a more fundamental, a more truly revolutionary, alteration
of its social structure: "All Europe is in a state of disturbance, of Revolution. . . . Their Parl. Reforms, and all that, are of small moment; a
beginning . . . nothing more. The whole frame of Society is rotten and
must go for fuel-wood" (*TNB*, 186, 183–84). Although he distrusted
the utilitarian principles of the philosophic radicals, he shared their
desire for radical reform, following the course of events in the *Examiner*, which he considered the "cleverest of all Radicals" (*CL*, 5:201;
see 249, 270).

In January, Carlyle read the first of a series of articles in the *Examiner*, entitled "Spirit of the Age," that seemed to support the ideas he
had set forth in the first draft of "Thoughts on Clothes." Like Carlyle,
its author was concerned with the problem of finding "authority which
commands confidence" during an "era of transition" (*Newspaper Writings*, 244). He also shared Carlyle's sense that they were living in an
era of revolution, that "the times are pregnant with change; and that
the nineteenth century will be known to posterity as the era of one
of the greatest revolutions of which history has preserved the remem-
brance" (230). He even employed the clothing metaphor to make the
point that revolution is the process by which society throws off outmoded institutions and "renovate[s]" itself: "Mankind have outgrown
old institutions and old doctrines, and have not yet acquired new ones.
When we say outgrown, we intend to prejudge nothing. A man may
not be either better or happier at six-and-twenty, than he was at six
years of age: but the same jacket which fitted him then, will not fit

him now" (230). On January 21 (the article appeared on January 9), Carlyle wrote his brother praising "Spirit of the Age"—he discovered in reply that its author was John Stuart Mill—and outlining for the first time his plans for extensively revising his essay on clothes (*CL*, 5:215–16, 235). Mill's essay seems to have encouraged him to expand "Thoughts on Clothes" and to seek a more serious outlet for it than Fraser's satirical literary magazine, to which he had originally submitted it. In March, while Parliament began considering the reform bill, he began to rework "Thoughts on Clothes," and in late July, while Parliament still sat in a state of indecision, he took the revised manuscript to London.

Like "The Spirit of the Age," *Sartor Resartus* addresses itself to and analyzes Carlyle's "revolutionary times," its opening chapter alluding directly to the Revolt of Paris and the British agitation for Reform (6). *Sartor Resartus* inscribes its origins in the Paris Revolt in its fictional frame where the "British Editor," who transcribes and narrates the life and opinions of Diogenes Teufelsdröckh, completes his work just at the moment when the "Parisian Three Days" begins (296). Furthermore, its central figure, the German clothes philosopher, is a "Radical" "Sansculottist" (63, 59).[4] *Sartor Resartus* represents a world in which ideas can "overturn . . . the whole old system of Society," in which a sansculottic philosopher can tailor or author a new suit of social clothing (118).

Carlyle could hardly have chosen a more appropriate figure than clothing to represent an era of revolution. Not only did the metaphor have a long religious and literary history and an association with political revolution through the term *sansculotte*, but clothing was also the chief product of the *industrial* revolution. The textile industry was the first to be extensively mechanized and brought under the factory system, and the social disruptions wrought by these changes played a major role in producing the social unrest that led to the movement for reform. Hard hit by the decline in the value of their labor—between 1814 and 1829, the price of a piece of handmade calico dropped from 6*s*. 6*d*. to 1*s*. 1*d*.—hand-loom weavers were among the most active participants in the intermittent riots and mob activities of the late eighteenth and early nineteenth centuries (Ashton, 81; Logue, 194).[5] Carlyle perceived the fine irony that the glut of cloth produced by the industrial revolution would not serve to clothe the nation but to strip it naked, that weavers of cloth were being pushed toward sansculottism.

Carlyle, via his clothes philosopher Teufelsdröckh, uses the weaving of cloth, or the sewing of a suit of clothes, to represent the process of authoring beliefs and institutions. His emphasis on clothing as woven textile plays on the root of the word *text—texere,* to weave.[6] Transcendental authority authors, weaves, or sews together the institutions and beliefs that constitute human society. Clothes are the medium through which the transcendental becomes visible in the finite world of human history: "Church-Clothes are, in our vocabulary, the Forms, the *Vestures,* under which men have at various periods embodied and represented for themselves the Religious Principle" (214). At the moment of their creation, clothes adequately represent or reveal the transcendental. Insofar as beliefs and institutions possess transcendental authority, they unite the authority to compel belief and to compel obedience, but because clothes, beliefs, and institutions are historical, they gradually lose their ability to manifest or represent transcendental authority. Carlyle represents this aspect of clothing by emphasizing that cloth is an organic material subject to wear and decay. The rags of old customs must be discarded in the "laystall," where they will decompose and become fertilizer for the "organic filaments" from which new cloth can be woven.

The clothing metaphor thus represents the fundamental historicity of cultural institutions and the inevitability of periodic revolution (see Dale, *Victorian Critic,* 299; Vanden Bossche, "Revolution and Authority," 277). Since nothing can prevent the processes of decay that destroy old clothing, *Sartor*'s pervasive organic imagery suggests that revolution and historical change are natural, noncataclysmic processes. Carlyle was aware, however, that many of his contemporaries thought it possible to patch up the old suits of clothing, to revive old beliefs and institutions instead of creating new ones. This patching up, however, would only repress the forces of change that would eventually break out in violent, rather than peaceful, revolution. Carlyle also uses the clothing metaphor to suggest the dangers that arise when clothing becomes *custom*ary or *habit*ual.[7] While clothing is theoretically transparent to the authority it reveals, it also covers and conceals it. *Sartor Resartus* suggests that the organic process that wears out clothes increases their opacity. When clothes become impediments to the recognition of authority rather than revelations of it, one is justified in stripping away and destroying them so that they can be replaced with new clothing. Teufelsdröckh does not flinch at the thought of destroying worn-out clothing. In fact, he positively delights in the sansculottic vision in which "the Clothes fly off the whole dramatic corps; and Dukes, Grandees, Bishops, Generals, Anointed Presence itself, every mother's son of them, stand straddling there, not a shirt on them" (61).

Yet vision in *Sartor Resartus* seeks to make the transcendental manifest through new clothes, not just to pierce through and destroy clothing. One might expect that stripping away the clothing that conceals transcendental authority would be the surest way of recovering that authority. This is the position of "Adamites," antinomian sects that seek to recover paradise by living, like Adam, without clothes and without laws. But, for the Carlyle of *Sartor Resartus*, the fall into history makes the divine inaccessible except through clothing. Consequently, while Teufelsdröckh is a "Sansculottist," he is no "Adamite" (60). The antinomian Adamites of the sixteenth and seventeenth centuries had argued that human law cannot displace divine law and therefore wanted to discard human law, to go naked; but Teufelsdröckh insists that only through clothing can we produce social order, that "Society is founded upon Cloth," that "without clothes" there would be no "Politeness, Polity, or even Police" (51, 64; see 41, 60). In fact, the *sansculottes*, modern-day Adamites, have left society naked, stripped of the beliefs and institutions that constitute the social order. Organic clothing, alive with transcendental presence, produces just social relationships in a world otherwise subject to the amoral and purely mechanical laws of raw nature, a universe that is "one huge, dead, immeasurable *Steam-engine*, rolling on, in its dead indifference, to grind [one] limb from limb. O the vast, gloomy, solitary Golgotha, and *Mill* of Death" (164; emphasis added). The metaphor of the mill—punning on the name of the leading utilitarian philosopher, James Mill, a "Motive-Millwright"—connects the natural order to the laissez-faire economics espoused by the utilitarians (159, 220–21; see 68, 117, 232). Human beings, without the social order provided by custom, would tear one another to pieces.[8] When human law no longer manifests transcendental authority, it cannot simply be destroyed: it must be replaced. Voltaire rightly destroys the "Mythus of the Christian Religion" because it is no longer a vital system of belief, but he falls into the Adamite heresy when he fails to "embody the divine Spirit of" Christianity "in a new Mythus, in a new vehicle and vesture" (163, 194).

When it comes to discovering who has authority to make new clothing, however, *Sartor Resartus* becomes ambiguous, divided between a

Goethe who would author a new mythus and a Napoleon who preaches his doctrine "through the cannon's throat" (178). The figure of the king, whose "authority from God" enables him to rule by "divine right," combines the authority to compel belief and to compel obedience because he excels in "Ken-ning (Cunning), or which is the same thing, Can-ning" (249). Because *Sartor Resartus* privileges "kenning," that is, knowledge and belief, from which "canning," social action and law, derives, the king is more likely to be a man of letters like Goethe than a politician like Napoleon. Indeed, in his notebook, Carlyle had claimed that the "only Sovereigns in this world in these days are the Literary men," and when he introduces the idea of "Hero-worship" in *Sartor Resartus*, he gives as an example of the hero, not a political figure, but Voltaire (*TNB*, 184; *SR*, 251).

Yet the figure of Voltaire raises the problem of how the man of letters can act ("can") as well as know ("ken"). Throughout *Sartor Resartus*, Carlyle expresses the anxiety that Teufelsdröckh's vocation will lead him to emulate, not Goethe, but Voltaire and Byron (192, 194). Employing the metaphor of building to describe the creation of a new social structure, *Sartor Resartus* articulates an opposition between those writers who create and those who destroy. While England needs a "Rebuilder" or an "Architect," not a "hodman," English utilitarianism is "calculated for destroying . . . not for rebuilding" (248, 105, 234).[9] Similarly, Voltaire fails because he possesses "Only a torch for burning, no hammer for building" (163). This suggests that already in *Sartor Resartus*, Carlyle was beginning to doubt whether the man of letters could build, could replace the man of religion. To become a man of letters was to participate in the industrial revolution—journalism as the industry of literature—that was undermining rather than establishing authority.[10]

Because the man of letters "kens" but cannot "can," Carlyle is attracted to the political hero, the Napoleon, who "can" but does not "ken." Although a *sansculotte*, Teufelsdröckh is also concerned with social control, with the ability to enforce belief in order to guarantee a just social order.[11] This tendency of hero-worship to slide toward authoritarianism, or at least hierarchy, remains muted in *Sartor Resartus* because *Sartor* frames its analysis of the era of revolution in terms of the problem of religious belief, not, as the later works would, in terms of the institution of democracy. Although Teufelsdröckh is a *sansculotte* interested in social reform, he articulates his concern for reform through a religious medium, the problem of the loss and recovery of faith. Although Carlyle became increasingly concerned with discovering heroic leadership rather than establishing religious belief, he would never fully abandon the idea that there could be "no permanent beneficent arrangement of affairs" until "*Religion,* the cement of *Society,*" was reestablished (*TNB,* 179). Furthermore, he would always be haunted by the question that arose even as he introduced the idea of hero-worship in *Sartor Resartus*: "Kings *do* reign by divine right, or not at all. The King that were God-appointed, would be an emblem of God, and could *demand* all obedience from us. *But where is that King?*" (*TNB,* 185; emphasis added in last sentence).

The Author as *Sansculotte*

While *Sartor Resartus* represents Diogenes Teufelsdröckh as a *sansculotte* who becomes an authority, its first readers were more ready to perceive its author as a revolutionary than an authority. The London publishers found it so unconventional that they would not risk publishing it while the political scene remained unsettled.[12] This rejection led Carlyle to doubt whether the man of letters could become an authority. The reaction of the publishers anticipated the reaction of friends like John Sterling, who objected that *Sartor*'s style was "barbarous" and "lawless," that its neologisms were "without any authority" (*SR,* 309–11).[13] Carlyle responded to the charge in the terms he had used to discuss revolution in *Sartor Resartus* itself: "If one has thoughts not hitherto uttered in English Books, I see nothing for it but that you must use words not found there, must *make* words." Arguing that "revolution" had already undermined "the whole structure of our Johnsonian' English," he defended a style that attempted to forge a new language in its place (*CL,* 8:135; see *TNB,* 264). Although born of his desire to "prophesy," to "make men hear [his] voice," *Sartor Resartus* remained unheard for two years while he worked toward a new conception of literature (*CL,* 5:43, *TNB,* 152).

What Sterling and the other critics sought was a point of reference, a shared or standard language, from outside of the text. Carlyle, too, sought a shared language, but found it necessary to create a new one because the old shared language had become meaningless. Consequently, the Carlylean hero is self-authorizing. Teufelsdröckh casts off the clothes, the profession and worldview, conferred on him by society, and determines to make his own clothes, to author his own myths. Whereas royal authority had been established with reference to a system of primogeniture external to itself, the hero's authority is established through his own ability.

As a result, *Sartor Resartus*, loaded with neologism and metaphor, is not only "hyper-metaphorical" but highly self-referential (293). Neologism and metaphor, a new word and the substitution of a new word or image for another, are both attempts to represent what cannot be represented through the existing vocabulary. Since Teufelsdröckh's language is, at least theoretically, entirely new, since it cannot obtain meaning by reference to any previous text, it must become entirely self-referential. The network of clothing metaphors in *Sartor Resartus* defines itself in relation to the network of organic metaphors, which in turn defines itself in relation to other networks of imagery, until they all become one vast, self-defining network. In fact, the web or network—as in the figure of weaving—is one of the principal metaphors of the book. Furthermore, any object or place that might appear to refer to some literal object outside of the symbolical pattern ultimately tends to be absorbed into the metaphorical network.[14] Finally, many of the textual practices that readers have found characteristic of *Sartor Resartus*—the dislocation of chronology, the use of character as "motif" or "general concept," the elaboration of binary oppositions, and the "multi-levelled fiction" in which the principal narrator edits and comments on writings by Teufelsdröckh and Hofrath Heuschrecke—all serve to intensify *Sartor*'s self-referentiality.[15]

Carlyle's early readers seemed to have been most concerned about this hermetic tendency of *Sartor Resartus*. A reader for one of the publishers that rejected it thought it "doubtful" that the work "would take with the public" (*CL*, 6:6, n. 1). Sterling complained that instead of employing familiar metaphors and fables, instead of using "Old" figures to present "New" ideas, Carlyle persisted in confronting the reader with tropes and figures that "the common reader must find perfectly bewildering" (*SR*, 311–12). Emerson, although among the earliest admirers of *Sartor*, reinforced Sterling's objections when he complained that its unfathomable diction seemed to indicate that the "Prophet . . . despair[ed] of finding a contemporary audience" (*RWE*, 98).[16] Carlyle acknowledged to both Emerson and Mill (who had made similar criticisms) that he had not gauged his audience adequately, concluding, "I never know or can even guess what or who my audience is, or whether I have any audience" (*CL*, 6:449; see 7:264–66).[17]

If authors are self-authorizing and their texts self-referential, they risk enclosing themselves in a private world cut off from their audience. Furthermore, because authors can provide no external signs of their authority, an audience has no way of distinguishing between an author with transcendental authority and a fraud. In *Sartor Resartus*, Carlyle appropriately uses George Fox, the founder of the Quakers (one of his encyclopedia articles was about them), to represent the self-authorizing author. Fox, like Teufelsdröckh, is a rebel who casts off "[m]ountains of encumbrance," the old clothes that constrain him, and stitches together his own "perennial suit of Leather . . . into one continuous all-including Case" that recuperates the "vesture . . . one and indivisible" of Teufelsdröckh's youth (210–11; 92). Fox's attempt to regain prelapsarian innocence represents Carlyle's desire to recover a transcendental language. But, although rebellion liberates Fox from his "Prison" into "lands of true Liberty," the language he speaks does not become a shared belief, a constitutive mythus; it remains private (211). Indeed, as early as "The State of German Literature," Carlyle had argued that mystics like Jacob Böhme and George Fox were "ignorant" of the state of their fellow human beings, speaking "not in the language of men, but of one man who had not learned the language of men" (*CME*, 1:73). An inheritor of the Enlightenment, Carlyle was well aware that the sincere mystic who claimed divine inspiration could just as easily be a deluded madman.

Carlyle saw this fate in the career of his close friend Edward Irving, a career that paralleled his own. Irving's more conventional vocation initially provided him with the authority that Carlyle longed for. His sermons so powerfully affected his listeners that in 1821, when Carlyle had not even begun his career as a writer, Irving was invited to London, where he found a large and enthusiastic audience. His ability to communicate with this audience seemed to expand when members of his congregation began speaking in tongues, the Old Testament image of the ideal shared language. But, in fact, the language was shared only by a small minority of Irving's followers, the majority deserting the congregation. No *philosophe* could have been more suspicious of religious "enthusiasts"—he identified Irving with the "ranters," a sect related to Fox's Quakers—than the Carlyle who concluded that speaking in tongues "was *no* special work of the Holy Spirit, or any Spirit save of that black frightful unclean one that dwells in Bedlam"; Irving must be self-deceived or a deceiver (*CL*, 6:41). Carlyle concluded in his obituary notice of 1835 that, instead of bringing religious belief to the public, Irving had "shut himself up in a lesser world of ideas and persons, and lived isolated there" (*CME*, 3:322; see *CL*, 6:65).[18]

It is only a short step from the self-deluded, like Irving and Fox, to those who intentionally delude others. If the James Carlyle of "The Reminiscence of James Carlyle" represents the author who possesses transcendental authority, Cagliostro, in an essay written one year later, represents the author who dupes his contemporaries with false claims of transcendental authority. Carlyle proposed the topic of "Count Cagliostro" to the editor of the *Edinburgh Review* just four months after his father's death (*CL*, 6:167). His interest in the topic must have been special, for it was one of the rare times in his early career that he was able to write for a review on a topic of his own choosing rather than one assigned by an editor. "Count Cagliostro" reflects on, even satirizes, Teufelsdröckh's discovery of authority in *Sartor Resartus*, suggesting that, while Teufelsdröckh seeks to become an "architect" who can build like the mason James Carlyle, he is in danger of becoming a charlatan "freemason" like Cagliostro.

Cagliostro's career parodies the career narrative Carlyle had constructed in his earlier writings. Cagliostro's family, against his will, arranges for him to become a monk, just as Carlyle's parents hoped he would become a minister. Like Carlyle, Cagliostro rejects this vocation, deciding instead to become an artist; but his only talent is for forgery, writing that deceives. Exiled from Palermo after the discovery of his crimes, Cagliostro becomes, like Teufelsdröckh, a wanderer in the eighteenth-century world of atheism and democracy. Just as Teufelsdröckh takes his nightly cup of beer at a coffee-house named "Zur Grünen Gans," Cagliostro spends a night at a fictitious inn named the "Green Goose" (*SR*, 15; *CME*, 3:279).[19] Driven by hunger to seek a profession, both become professors and discourse on "Things in General," though Teufelsdröckh is a "Professor of Things in General" and Cagliostro a "Professor of Swindlery" (*SR*, 120, 18; *CME*, 3:268, 292). Both observe the world from a metaphorical "watch-tower," and just as Teufelsdröckh promises a "new mythus," the *Palingensia* that will bring a "Newbirth of Society," Cagliostro claims that he brings a new "Evangel" that will "Renovat[e] . . . the Universe" (*SR*, 6, 20, 217; *CME*, 3:262, 286). Yet *Sartor*, playful as it is, never questions Teufelsdröckh's sincerity, or even his ability to author a *Palingensia*, while "Count Cagliostro" never permits us to believe its hero is anything but a quack.

Nonetheless, in ridiculing Cagliostro's claims to possess the authority of a James Carlyle and emphasizing his similarity to Teufelsdröckh, the essay implicitly questions Teufelsdröckh's project, suggesting that he may be as self-deluded as Irving or Fox. Insisting on his transcendental authority, Cagliostro claims to be God's "chosen . . . apostle," to possess "authority over the Angels," and to act by "the power of God" (*CME*, 3:293, 287). As "Renovator of the Universe," he promises to restore the world to a "primitive state of innocence, lost by original sin," a transcendental idyll (286). But, whereas James Carlyle had built his idyllic home out of stone, Cagliostro builds his "Masonic hall" of "gilt-pasteboard"; whereas Carlyle represents his father's creations as permanent and substantial, he represents Cagliostro's as theatrical illusions no more substantial than "foam" or "soap-bubble[s]" (*CME*, 3:291, 285; see Campbell, "Edward Irving").

Most importantly, the representation of Cagliostro's language parodies Teufelsdröckh's, revealing how distant Teufelsdröckh is from James Carlyle. Just as Cagliostro's theatrical freemasonry is the opposite of James Carlyle's substantial masonry, his "froth-speeches" are the opposite of the elder Carlyle's potent words (*CME*, 3:285). As opposed to the unitary prelapsarian language of James Carlyle, Cagliostro's dialect, composed of "Sicilian-Italian, and Laquais-de-Place French, garnished with shreds from all European dialects," seems almost a parody of *Sartor* and its heavy doses of German (*CME*, 3:293). His speech is simply a parody of Teufelsdröckh's "sleeping and soporific passages; *circumlocutions*, repetitions, touches even of pure doting *jargon*": Cagliostro "babble[s] in long-winded diffusions, chaotic *circumvolutions* tending nowhither . . . a Tower-of-Babel *jargon*. . . . His whole thought is confused, inextricable; what thought, what resemblance of thought he has, cannot deliver itself, except in gasps, blustering gushes, spasmodic refluences, which make bad worse" (*SR*, 31; *CME*, 3:293; emphasis added). Both speak the fragmented language of a post-Babelian era of unbelief.

Cagliostro's inverse creation, "working the mighty chaos, into a creation—of ready-money," similarly parodies Teufelsdröckh's intention to imitate the god of Genesis who creates paradise out of the primordial chaos (*CME*, 3:291; *SR*, 197). Cagliostro is a counterfeit prophet:

"If the ancient Father was named Chrysostom, or Mouth-of-Gold, be the modern Quack named Pinchbecko-stom, or Mouth-of-Pinchbeck" (*CME*, 3:296). Saint John Chrysostom, who was reputed to be the greatest orator of the early church, was persecuted for speaking plainly about the faults of governors and wrote biblical commentaries that emphasized literal meaning and practical applications. Whereas Chrysostom's words, as his name indicates, have the value of gold, Cagliostro's are pinchbeck—that is to say, counterfeit. Instead of using his mouth to act upon the world creatively, Cagliostro survives through "Eatableness, and Similitude of Doing"; he is a "raven," a "bustard," a "jackal," a predator who feeds on the victims drawn to him by his delusive words (*CME*, 3:318, 269, 284, 306; see 261, 263, 274, 300). "Count Cagliostro" represents Carlyle's anxiety that instead of leading his readers into the promised land, he was leading them to a "gilt-pasteboard" paradise.[20]

From Craigenputtoch to London

In 1828, Carlyle had attempted to recover the domestic idyll by moving from Edinburgh to Craigenputtoch, a farm on the remote moors of southwest Scotland. Edinburgh represented urban exile, exclusion from the family and its religious faith, even loss of health. His chronic dyspepsia—probably a psychosomatic manifestation of his spiritual crisis—first developed while he was living there, and he came to feel that he could only recover physical as well as spiritual health by returning to the country. He had been reduced to hackwork and prevented from pursuing the higher calling of literature. From this time, Carlyle tended to identify English literature as the hack production of urban industry—he depicted the literary men of London as a "rascal rout, [a] dirty rabble" (*CL*, 3:234)—while idealizing the literature of Germany. His preference for calling advertising "puffery" emphasized his conception of it as giving a false illusion of significance to what was in reality without meaning or value. Yet he, too, was enmeshed in the network of commerce. When he saw his own name advertised in the windows of the *Athenæum* offices, he chided himself in his notebook for contributing to the journal: "Why yield even half a hair's-breadth to Puffing? Abhor it, utterly divorce it, and kick it to the Devil!" (*TNB*, 233; see *CME*, 3:101). Indeed, the treatment of literature as a mere commodity was nowhere more evident than in the pages of the *Athenæum*, where advertisements for books appeared alongside those for hair oil and patent medicines.[21]

Yet escape from the toils of urban industry was not easy. Carlyle had already attempted to recover the childhood idyll in 1825, the year he spent on a farm at Hoddam Hill. Symbolically reunited with his family—his mother spent part of the year there—he felt as if he was in his "second boyhood," able to escape time and recover the oceanic timelessness that Teufelsdröckh would ascribe to his "Idyllic" childhood: "Time no longer hurries past me like a mountain flood, the channel of which is soon to lie dead and empty: it spreads around me like a placid sea" (*CL*, 3:330, 349; *SR*, 90; see Kaplan, 111ff.). Late the following year he married Jane Welsh, and they settled in Edinburgh, where he tried but failed to write the two novels "Illudo Chartis" and *Wotton Reinfred*. By 1828, Edinburgh had come to represent not only the loss of family, faith, and health, but the corruption of literature by the publishing industry.

Unable to write a work of his own and wracked with dyspepsia, both moral and physical, he began to insist that only the country could cure him (*CL*, 4:198–99, 233, 359). Craigenputtoch, like Hoddam Hill, would be an Eden, a "green oasis," where he could recapture health and become an authority. Because they could live at Craigenputtoch cheaply—Jane Carlyle had inherited the property from her father—he would "not be tempted to tell lies for money" and could "cultivate Literature" (*CL*, 4:407–8). He became fond of comparing Craigenputtoch to Patmos, the island in the Aegean where Saint John wrote the book of Revelations, a place to write "mystical *Reviews*" and to begin "prophesying" (*CL*, 4:434). In a more sportive mood, he suggested that it might even become an idyll for literary men, like the one he had imagined as the House in the Wold in *Wotton Reinfred* (see *CL*, 5:433). Although this proposal to create an idyll populated by writers rather than shepherds was partly tongue-in-cheek, Carlyle was serious when he insisted that in his "rustic solitude . . . the business of magazine-writing and the profits and disprofits of magazine conducting are utterly alien" (*CL*, 4:106).[22]

But he came to associate the very conditions that made writing *Sartor Resartus* possible—social isolation and freedom from the marketplace—with its transcendental solipsism. Jane Carlyle hated Craigenputtoch because of its social isolation, and Carlyle came to regard it less as a refuge than as a prison. During his visit to London in 1831–32, he had still been able to look back to Craigenputtoch as a fortress within which he could retreat to safety from the Babylonian city (*CL*, 5:429–30, 6:64). When he failed to sell *Sartor Resartus*, he began to disparage Craigenputtoch and to contemplate a move to London. The country had not cured him of his urban dyspepsia, and by January 1833 he had decided that Craigenputtoch was no longer a "wholesome" abode (*CL*, 6:291, 308, 330). By the time he and Jane decided to move to London in 1834, he saw the change as his "*last* chance . . . to redeem [his] existence from Pain and Imprisonment," as breaking out of a "Bastille" (*CL*, 7:104, 124).

Carlyle had come to regard Craigenputtoch, not as withstanding the invading world of commerce as his childhood home had done, but as imprisoning him, preventing his prophecies from reaching the world because it isolated him from the social community represented by the people he met during his stay in London. When Mill, Emerson, and Sterling complained that he did not seem to take his audience into account, he blamed the solitude of Craigenputtoch, where he had been unable to envision his audience because he had "no known public" and was "*alone* under the Heavens" (*CL*, 7:265). He no longer depicted Craigenputtoch as a land of plenty but as a barren place incapable of producing literature: "Nothing ever was more ungenial than the soil that poor Teufelsdröckhish seedcorn has been thrown on here" (*CL*, 7:264). The "green oasis" he had described to Goethe in 1828 had by 1834 turned into the "Dunscore Desert . . . a place doomed, even in my memory, to silence, obstruction, and the dispiritment of motionless desolation; a place I care not if I never see again!" (*CL*, 4:407, 7:280). It would seem the problem with Craigenputtoch was precisely its idyllic timelessness, an "everlasting Solitude" in which there was "no human soul with which to commune" (*CL*, 7:112; 6:210).

So, instead of escaping the constraints of the literary marketplace, Carlyle had only cut himself off from the source of his income. He still needed to write reviews to survive, and, in spite of economies, found in February 1831, as he set out to revise *Sartor Resartus*, that he had only "some £5 to front the world with" (*TNB*, 183). His realization that he was writing for an urban market impelled him to take the manuscript of *Sartor Resartus* to London, and his experience there made even clearer to him the importance of staying in contact with the editors who controlled the publishing industry. Although *Sartor* was rejected, he returned to Craigenputtoch with "plenty" of commissions from editors he had met during his stay (*CL*, 6:131). In the immensely productive year between his father's death in January 1832 and his decision to leave Craigenputtoch in January 1833, he wrote eight articles, translated Goethe's "Novelle," and wrote an introduction to his translation of Goethe's "Das Märchen," these pieces appearing in *Fraser's*, the *Edinburgh Review*, the *Foreign Quarterly Review*, the *Monthly Magazine*, and the *New Monthly Magazine*. With "Characteristics," which was "approved seemingly by every one whose approval was wanted," he seemed finally to have discovered his audience (*CL*, 6:132).

As the year drew on, however, Carlyle's distance from London told (*CL*, 6:138). After the first round of articles, he received no further commissions, except from Fraser, who published six of his pieces in 1832 and would be the only editor to publish his work in 1833. "My whole trade is to think and *speak*," he complained to Mill, "but as the world goes, I have absolutely no permission to speak! Think of poor *me* and poor *Fraser's Magazine*! Yet such is my *best* speaking-mechanism at this moment; for aught I know, it is my only one" (*CL*, 7:25). He considered *Fraser's*, which always took his work but paid poorly, a "Dog's-meat Cart," "a chaotic, fermenting, dung-hill heap of compost" that had "*nothing* to do" with "*Literature*" (*TNB*, 232, 259, 170). He longed to free himself not only from *Fraser's*, but from all connection with journalism, yet, with *Sartor Resartus* languishing in manuscript, he was forced to continue with it: "One must write 'Articles'," he lamented, "write and curse" (*CL*, 6:265).

At this point, London came to represent the possibility of producing for an audience that acknowledged his authority. While he might still regard London as a "Phlegethon-Fleetditch," he now concluded that literature could not "be carried on elsewhere by an Englishman" (*CL*, 7:142). During his 1831–32 visit to London, he had found "great respect, even love from some few." As he recalled these admirers in the isolation of Craigenputtoch, London began to look "more and more poetic," a more "natural" situation than the rural "wilderness" (*CL*, 7:177, 280; see 6:126).

Yet, if moving to London brought him into contact with his audience and the marketplace, Carlyle still needed to discover a literary form through which to address them. Like Schiller, in addition to moving to the commercial center, he turned to history, a form that "would . . . afford him . . . the necessary competence of income" (*LS*, 85). Whereas he had sought publishers for *Sartor Resartus* and his book on German literature for years without success, it took only one month to settle with a publisher for his history of the French Revolution even though he had not yet written a word of it.

From Transcendental Novel to Epic History

At the same time that he was moving from Craigenputtoch to London, Carlyle was shifting his concept of the literary text from the transcendental novel toward epic history. After the crisis of 1832, he began to seek a new form that would enable him to overcome the shortcomings of *Sartor Resartus*. The "great maxim" of his father's philosophy, he had written in "The Reminiscence of James Carlyle," was "That man was created to work, not to speculate, or feel, or dream" (5). Yet in *Sartor Resartus* he had written a book founded on dreams and speculation rather than the "*practical* and real" enjoined by his father (18). In "On Biography," the first essay he wrote after the death of his father, he criticized novelists for revealing "Nothing but a pitiful Image of their own pitiful Self, with its vanities, and grudgings, and ravenous hunger of all kinds" (*CME*, 3:58; see 49).[23] Since he had always thought of the artwork he longed to create as a novel—he once described *Sartor* as a "Didactic Novel"—this statement marks a significant alteration in his conception of the literary work (*CL*, 6:396). Instead, he would now create an epic, for epics, in contrast to novels, were "Histories, and understood to be narratives of *facts*" (*CME*, 3:49–50).[24]

Carlyle's representation of epic had as much to do with contemporary Homeric scholarship as with Homer's works and the epic tradition.[25] In the late eighteenth and early nineteenth centuries, scholars were seeking to replace the conception of Homer as the "ideal ancient sage" with the "historically plausible ancient poet: a representative or even a colletive name for the Greek people in their most primitive stage of development" (Grafton et al., 10). Like biblical scholars and students of folk literature, they were abandoning the idea that these texts were authored by individuals, as modern poems were.[26] When Carlyle compared the *Iliad* to a collection of "ballad delineations" like the legends of Robin Hood (which had been edited by Ritson in 1795), he was only echoing what was by then the commonplace that Homer's writings were collections of "songs and rhapsodies" produced by generations of "folk" (*HL*, 16).[27] Friedrich Wolf, who was at the forefront of this movement, argued further that the *Iliad* had been created by collecting songs composed in a preliterate era (Turner, 138–47; see Foerster, 59–60, 72–73).[28] Consequently, the collectors who gathered the songs were more like editors than authors, as the materials came from a body of already existing folk material, not from their own imaginations (Myres, 49, 86). Under the influence of this movement, the idea that the Homeric epics were, like the Bible, not works of imaginative fiction but repositories of folk beliefs about the nature of the universe and a history of a people, became commonplace (Turner, 140, 154; Jenkyns, 197, 204; Myres, 81).[29] Typical was Wolf's mentor, Christian Heyne, who, as Carlyle observed, "read in the writings of the Ancients . . . their spirit and character, their way of life and thought" (*CME*, 1:351).[30] This understanding of Homer underlay Carlyle's assertion in "On Biography" that "All Mythologies were once Philosophies; were *believed:* the Epic Poems of old time, so long as they continued *epic* . . . were Histories, and understood to be narratives of *facts*" (*CME*, 3:49–50).[31]

Epic, as Carlyle represents it, fulfills his claim that literature could replace religion. The canons by which Carlyle decided that a text was an epic had more to do with whether the text functioned as a sacred work than with whether it possessed all the formal characteristics of epic. In "On Biography," he claimed that, along with the *Iliad*, the Hindu scriptures (the *Shaster*) and the Koran were the most authentic epics (*CME*, 3:51). He considered a text like the *Nibelungenlied* a "Northern Epos" or "German Iliad" because it was "common property and plebian," a foundational cultural text that was widely read and believed (*CME*, 2:270, 218). He did not attempt to explain how the people acquired this belief or the process of inspiration that gave these texts transcendental authority, but, by extending the scholarly analogy between the *Iliad* and the Bible, he suggested that epic history is a form of revelation.

The second half of Carlyle's statement in "On Biography," that epics were "histories"—a statement in keeping with the widely held belief that the Homeric poems were historical—suggests that epics manifest belief as it is enacted in history (Turner, 136–37). He argued that we discover the beliefs of the Greeks not in what they said, but in how they acted, the history of their actions in the war with Troy. The epic poet would be a historian who records not what he imagines, like the novelist, but the history of his culture, like Homer. By the time Carlyle wrote "The Diamond Necklace" in 1833, he had redefined poetry, particularly epic poetry, as history, and history as poetry: "The story of the *Diamond Necklace* is all told . . . with the strictest fidelity; yet in a kind of *musical* way: it seems to me there is no Epic possible that does not first of all ground itself on Belief" (*CL*, 7:61; see *CME*, 3:329).

Carlyle had not always regarded history as epic or revelation. His youthful enthusiasm for history reflected little more than a cultural bias against fiction shared by Calvinists and utilitarians alike (see *CL*, 1:354–55). In the early 1820s, he did not even consider history a literary form.[32] After the Leith Walk experience of 1822 and his discovery of Goethe and Schiller, literature completely replaced history in his praises; from 1823 until he began reading up on the French Revolution in 1832, his letters, which had previously recommended long lists of histories, hardly mention them. By 1830, when he wrote "Thoughts on History," however, he had begun to consider history an art. His second essay on history ("Quae Cogitavit" [1833], now known as "On History Again") went further, arguing, under the influence of the Germans, that history was the primary form of knowledge: "All Books, therefore, were they but Song-books or treatises on Mathematics, are in the long run historical documents. . . . History is not only the fittest study, but the only study, and includes all others whatsoever" (*CME*, 3:167–68). Carlyle no longer regarded history as an alternative to fiction or literature, but as the fundamental literary form.

Carlyle's model for the epic historian is the editor or collector who gathers songs and rhapsodies together in a single text. In *On Heroes and Hero-Worship*, he was to argue that Dante did not create his epic through a private act of imagination, but set down the beliefs of his culture: the *Divine Comedy*, he wrote, "belongs to ten Christian centuries, only the finishing of it is Dante's" (*HHW*, 98). Similarly, *Reinecke Fuchs* is a collective myth "fashion[ed] . . . together" from two centuries of European culture (*CME*, 2:322, 275). Just as there was no single Homer or Moses who authored the *Iliad* and the Pentateuch, so there was "no single author" who created *Reinecke Fuchs* or the mythus of Christianity embodied in *The Divine Comedy*. The single author who sets out self-consciously to create an epic by employing epic machinery and epic form, but does not believe in the epic myth, will fail. Carlyle's principal criterion for inclusion in or exclusion from the epic canon is whether or not the author is "fatal[ly] conscious" that he is writing an epic (*HL*, 52). On this basis, he includes the Bible, the *Iliad*, the *Shaster*, the Koran, the *Nibelungenlied*, *Reinecke Fuchs*, *The Divine Comedy*, and Ebenezer Elliot's "Enoch Wray," but excludes the *Aeneid*, the *Lusiad*, the *Epigoniad*, and *Paradise Lost*. In fact, for Carlyle, epics begin to lose their epic status once they are written down. When editors decide to collect and record epic songs, they have become conscious that an epic exists; only when epic retains its origins as unselfconscious song, when it remains musical (i.e., oral), can a poem be truly epic (*HGL*, 63; *HL*, 22).[33]

Thus, Carlyle attempted to solve the hermeneutic dilemma of historical interpretation through the figure of the historian as editor who composes an epic out of a collection of songs and rhapsodies. In "On History," he had argued that the Enlightenment idea of history as "philosophy teaching by experience" assumed that experience presents no problems of interpretation, and countered that "Before philosophy can teach by Experience, the Philosophy has to be in readiness, the Experience be gathered and intelligibly recorded" (*CME*, 2:85). Since experience requires interpretation, writing history becomes the process of interpreting the texts that constitute the historical record. In "On History Again," he represents historians as continuously interpreting and reinterpreting the historical record: "Thus, do not the records of a Tacitus acquire new meaning, after seventeen hundred years, in the hands of a Montesquieu?" (*CME*, 3:175). Whereas the fictitious Editor of *Sartor Resartus* had patched together the life and opinions of Teufelsdröckh out of his own speculations like a novelist, the historian, like Dante or Homer, patches together epic history out of the recorded experiences and activities of a culture. As he put it in "Cagliostro," the quack works in "the element of Wonder" and the "infinitude of the Unknown"; the "Genuine . . . artist or artisan, works in the finitude of the Known" (*CME*, 3:296).

The drive toward transcendence as a recuperation of home in *Sartor Resartus* had instead returned Carlyle to the prison of solipsism. Paradoxically, in order to commune with fellow human beings, he had to become alienated from the transcendental totality of the family idyll, to discover himself as historically contingent. This is not to say, however, that Carlyle's move to London and his subsequent writings enabled him to avoid the potential authoritarianism that may cause individuals seeking to force others to accept their transcendental authority to turn against one another. The drive to achieve transcendence in *Sartor Resartus* would persist in his histories (see Ragland-Sullivan, 272).

Carlyle's idealist conception of history as revelation tends to negate historical time.[34] Since history records enacted belief, and beliefs are authored by transcendental authority, Carlyle represented history as revelation (*CME*, 2:94, 3:53–54, 176, 250; *SR*, 177, 254; see Moore, "Carlyle and Fiction" 135ff.; Shine, *Carlyle's Fusion of Poetry*, 55–56; Baker, 35–37; Sigman, 252; J. Rosenberg, 49–51; McGowan, chap. 3). Yet epic history can possess transcendental authority only insofar as it coincides with a divine order that is itself ahistorical. This coincidence would exist for only a moment because the historical development of beliefs and institutions always moves away from ahistorical authority. Nonetheless, Carlyle never took the final step leading him to a more radical historicism that would regard even temporary coincidence of transcendental authority and historical form illusory.

Rather, he shared with his contemporaries a tendency to regard history as moving toward a state of ahistorical transcendence. Even in Mill's "Spirit of the Age," as well as the St. Simonian writings on which it was based, Carlyle found corroboration for the cyclical model of history that he had found in the writings of the Germans, a temporal cycle in which "transitional" and "natural" states of society alternate (*Newspaper Writings*, 252).[35] These models of history are not dialectical; they hypostatize the elements of cultural consensus of certain eras in order to posit epochs of "nature," "belief," or "culture," while they treat historical change as characteristic only of intermediate periods of "transition," "unbelief," or "anarchy." The former are idyllic and timeless states, like Teufelsdröckh's childhood or his transcendence of time and space in the Everlasting Yea. History is confined to the transitional period that by its nature is regarded as having no coherence or center. This model tends to posit three stages, a period of unbelief or transition coming between periods of belief or nature; one never finds the cycle represented in the converse manner, as a period of cultural consensus sandwiched between two periods of change. Carlyle and his contemporaries universally considered themselves to be living in a period of transition; in effect, they felt that they lived in an era saturated with history, overwhelmed by time. Able to discover transcendence only in the past, they envisioned history as moving out of itself toward a future belief, nature, culture—a renewed transcendence that escapes history (see Houghton, *Victorian Frame*, 1–4).[36]

In the essays following "On Biography"—"Boswell's Life of Johnson," "Diderot," "Count Cagliostro," and "The Diamond Necklace"—

Carlyle followed Schiller's path from "the love of contemplating or painting things as they should be"—the metaphysical speculations of *Sartor Resartus*—to "the love of knowing things as they are"—to history (*LS*, 84). Since epic must record the beliefs of an epoch as they are enacted in its history, Carlyle would turn to the history of his own era, more specifically, the eighteenth century, the era in which history and revolution asserted themselves and destroyed the transcendental idyll. The sequence of essays he wrote during this period moves from Johnson, who nearly escapes history, to Cagliostro and the principals of the Diamond Necklace affair, who are at one with the era.

The essay on Johnson, written soon after James Carlyle's death, was virtually a tribute to Carlyle's father.[37] Both Johnson and James Carlyle, as Carlyle represents them, resisted the historical tendencies of their time, sustaining religious belief in an atheistic era (*Rem.*, 10; *CME*, 3:89, 105). The anecdote in which Carlyle recalls how Johnson had atoned for slighting his father also represents Carlyle's desire to atone for writing fiction, which his father had considered "*false* and criminal" (*CME*, 3:129–30; *Rem.*, 9). When he writes that Johnson never rose into "the region of Poetic art," he is not demeaning his literary achievements but shifting allegiance from poetry to prose; the only "Poetry" his father liked, the reminiscence records, was "Truth and the Wisdom of Reality" (*CME*, 3:126; *Rem.*, 8). Just two months after finishing "Boswell's Johnson," Carlyle was advising Ebenezer Elliot to exchange his rhymes for prose, and from this time forward he recommended prose, the medium of "reality," over verse, the medium of speculation (*CME*, 3:165).

After the essay on Johnson, Carlyle turned to figures who are embedded in the history of the French eighteenth century. Whereas Johnson resisted the process of historical change, his contemporary Diderot contributed to the general progress of decay. Rather than a godlike authority who pierces through immediate circumstances to the transcendental, Diderot is constituted by and limited to his own historical circumstances: the "most gifted soul appearing in France of the Eighteenth Century . . . thinks of the things belonging to the French eighteenth century, and in the dialect he has learned there" (*CME*, 3:229). Cagliostro is not only determined by historical circumstances, he has no self apart from them (see Vanden Bossche, "Fictive Text"). The lives of empty illusion led by Cagliostro, Cardinal de Rohan, Marie Antoinette, the Countess Lamotte, and the other participants in the Diamond Necklace affair reflect an era in which substance has disappeared and only the surface of history remains. "The Diamond Necklace" concludes with an apocalyptic vision of the destruction of this history-bound world of imposture, a prophecy of the French Revolution.

Just four days after he announced his intention to leave Craigenputtoch while working on "Cagliostro" in January 1833, Carlyle sent Mill a request for a long list of books on the French Revolution (*CL*, 6:302). Throughout 1833, he read extensively on the revolution, steadily becoming convinced that he should write a history of it. In September, he wrote to Mill that it seemed to him "as if the right *History* . . . of the French Revolution were the grand Poem of our Time; as if the man who *could* write the *truth* of that, were worth all other writers and singers" (*CL*, 6:446). In October, he further expanded his idea of epic history: "One of the questions that oftenest presents itself, is *How* Ideals do and *ought to* adjust themselves with the Actual? . . . my value for the Actual (in all senses), for what *has realized* itself continues and increases: and often I ask myself, Is not all Poetry the essence of Reality . . . and true History the only possible Epic?" (*CL*, 7:24). His history of the French Revolution would attempt to represent the process through which, as the title of the second chapter of his history ("Realised Ideals") was to indicate, a people tried to realize a new ideal, a new belief. Two months later, while working on "The Diamond Necklace," his "first . . . experiment" at writing poetical history, he claimed that he was trying to see "whether by sticking actually to the Realities of the thing with as much tenacity and punctuality as the merest Hallam, one could not in a small way make a kind of Poem of it" (*CL*, 7:266, 57; see 61).

Having determined to write an epic history, he now sought to prepare himself by a close study of the *Iliad*, which Schiller had deemed a "model" epic (*LS*, 119). During the first four months of 1834, he read four books of the *Iliad*, perhaps more, in Greek, and the entire poem in Johann Voss's German translation along with the commentaries of Christian Heyne, Richard Payne Knight, and Thomas Blackwell.[38] As he began his Homer studies, he heard that *Sartor Resartus* was meeting "with the most unqualified disapproval" and subsequently learned that one of *Fraser's* oldest subscribers threatened to cancel his subscription "If there [was] any more of that d——d stuff" (*CL*, 7:81, 175; see 125, 139). If Carlyle had had any doubts about the change of direction he had taken, he now set them aside. He moved to London in May 1834 and soon after began working on *The French Revolution*. Writing now with an eye toward his audience, he observed happily that Jane found it a "more readable kind of Book" than *Sartor Resartus* and became confident it would be "Quite an Epic Poem of the Revolution" (*CL*, 7:314, 306).

The French Revolution as Symbolic History

Carlyle's ascription of the authorship of "On History Again" to Diogenes Teufelsdröckh suggests that the *Palingenesia*, a mythus intended to enable the rebirth of his society, would take the form of epic history. The French Revolution manifested the fundamental beliefs of Carlyle's own era just as the Trojan wars manifested the beliefs of the Greeks. Yet this subject was problematical because the revolution did more to destroy antiquated beliefs than to bring new beliefs to life; the only belief his society retained was the belief in unbelief that prevented him from authoring the new mythus promised in *Sartor Resartus*. Instead of creating a text that would bring about the birth of a new society, he would demonstrate how the revolution continued to be reborn in his own era, in the Paris Revolt of 1830 and the Reform Bill of 1832. Sansculottism "still lives," he was to write in the conclusion of *The French Revolution*, "still works far and wide . . . as is the way of Cunning Time with his New-Births" (3:311). By concluding his history of the revolution with the events of October 1795, just two months before his birth on December 4, 1795, Carlyle suggested that he himself was the first rebirth of the revolution, that it had indeed invaded the households of the lowly (*Rem.*, 30).[39] If it was an "unhappiness to be born" in such an era, to be a rebirth of its spirit, a history of the revolution would at least help one figure out "what to make of" the "age," what it means to be born of revolution (*FR*, 1:11; *HHW*, 201).

Carlyle's problem in writing *The French Revolution* was how to make it epic rather than novelistic in the sense that he used these terms in "On Biography." He wanted to avoid the problems raised by *Sartor Resartus*, especially that of his own authority, but he could not solve this problem simply by effacing the authorial ego. Indeed, the narrator of *The French Revolution* is every bit as prominent as the Editor of *Sartor Resartus*. Instead, Carlyle made himself into a narrator who interprets a society. He did not write *The French Revolution* as a factual chronology of political events but as a sequence of symbolic episodes through which the narrator, and the reader, discover the meaning of their own era. For this purpose, he shaped a unique historical narrator who speaks in the first person and present tense, represents the voices of the historical actors, and interprets symbols in order to create a double narrative, both epic and mock epic, of the revolution.[40]

The Editor of *Sartor Resartus* and the narrator of *The French Revolution* both represent themselves as interpreters. The Editor of *Sartor* must make sense of the "chaos" of the clothes volume and the six paper bags filled with random autobiographical fragments; the narrator of *The French Revolution* must contend with an intransigent imbroglio of historical documents. Each addresses the reader directly, setting himself the task of enabling the reader to make sense of this material. Yet *The French Revolution* reverses the procedure of *Sartor Resartus*. While the Editor begins with random symbols that he situates in a narrative framework of his own devising, the narrator of *The French Revolution* begins with a narrative chronology in which he must discover symbols.

The Editor attempts to explain the clothes philosophy and the life of Teufelsdröckh through narrative even though, as he represents it, the basic material of *Sartor Resartus* resists chronological narration. *Sartor* does not present a logical argument that develops from chapter to chapter; material from the first book could even be interchanged with material from the last (Levine, *Boundaries*, 41–43; see Gilbert, 433–36; Vanden Bossche, "Prophetic Closure," 212–13). The autobiographical fragments, from which the Editor constructs book 2, arrive in hardly any chronological, certainly no narrative, order. The patterns that the Editor uses to organize these materials do not inhere in them, but are familiar narrative paradigms that he imposes on them. To represent the process of coming to understand the clothes volume, for example, he employs the convention of the journey. Similarly, he fits the random autobiographical fragments to the conventional pattern of spiritual autobiography (see Peterson, 49–57). To the Editor, both the clothes volume and the life of Teufelsdröckh are a chaos that must be interpreted, but the interpretation appears to come from the preexisting narrative patterns he employs rather than from the materials themselves. Like the novelist in "On Biography," the Editor creates narratives that are "Nothing but a pitiful Image of [his] own pitiful Self" (*CME*, 3:58). Because there is no original text, only an interpretation of a fictitious text, *Sartor Resartus* represents the tendency of interpretation to overwhelm the interpreted text.

The narrator of *The French Revolution* finds most of his historical materials already arranged in chronological order in collections like the *Histoire Parlementaire* and the volumes of the *Moniteur*, but simply composing a chronological narrative would not enable him to discover the meaning of those events. He complains, furthermore, that the editors of the *Histoire Parlementaire* have already imposed a narrative depicting the recuperation of Christianity and counters: "But what if History were to admit, for once, that all the Names and Theorems yet known to her fall short? . . . In that case, History, renouncing the pretension to *name* it at present, will *look* honestly at it, and name what she can of it!" (3:204). Although Carlyle's history also has a thesis, he claims that he discovers it in the symbolic structure of the revolution itself. As opposed to *Sartor*'s Editor and the editors of the *Histoire Parlementaire* who derive their narrative patterns from preexisting narratives, Carlyle's narrator attempts to derive his interpretation from something outside of himself, from the historical material itself.

Because the narrator of *The French Revolution* can be regarded as a character whose role it is to interpret the history of the revolution, Carlyle does not employ the omniscient mode of historical narration, but a first-person mode that dramatizes the continuing process of interpretation. The conventional omniscient mode—using the third person and past tense to make history seem to "speak itself"—creates the illusion of objectivity by treating the past as fixed and the narrator's interpretation of it as exhaustive (Barthes, "Le Discours de l'histoire," 68).[41] In fact, omniscient narrative only disguises the presence of a first-person narrator and that narrator's ideological assumptions. Carlyle's use of the first person and present tense makes his presence explicit. We can see the difference between these two modes of history in the following narratives of the procession of the Assembly of Notables on May 4, 1789, the first from Archibald Alison's *History of Europe from the Commencement of the French Revolution in 1789 to the Restoration of the Bourbons in 1815* (1833) and the second from Carlyle's *French Revolution*:

> On the evening before [May 5, 1789], a religious ceremony preceded the installation of the Estates. The King, his family, his ministers, and the deputies of the three orders, walked in procession from the

church of Notre Dame to that of St. Louis, to hear mass. The appearance of the assembled bodies, and the reflection that a national solemnity, so long fallen into disuse, was about to be revived, excited the most lively enthusiasm in the multitude. The weather was fine; the benevolent and dignified air of the King, the graceful manners of the Queen, the pomp and splendour of the ceremony, and the undefined hopes which it excited, exalted the spirits of all who witnessed it. But the reflecting observed with pain, that the sullen lines of feudal etiquette were preserved with rigid formality, and they augured ill of the national representation which commenced its labours with such distinction. First marched the clergy in grand costume, with violet robes; next the noblesse, in black dresses, with gold vests, lace cravats, and hats adorned with white plumes; last, the Tiers Etat, dressed in black, with short cloaks, muslin cravats, and hats without feathers. But the friends of the people consoled themselves with the observation, that, however humble their attire, the numbers of this class greatly preponderated over those of the other orders. (1:181–82)[42]

Behold, however! The doors of St. Louis Church flung open; and the Procession of Processions advancing towards Notre-Dame! Shouts rend the air; one shout, at which Grecian birds might drop dead. It is indeed a stately, solemn sight. The Elected of France, and then the Court of France; they are marshalled and march there, all in prescribed place and Costume. Our Commons 'in plain black mantle and white cravat'; Noblesse, in gold-worked, bright-dyed cloaks of velvet, resplendent, rustling with laces, waving with plumes; the Clergy in rochet, alb, or other best *pontificalibus:* lastly comes the King himself, and King's Household, also in their brightest blaze of pomp,—their brightest and final one. Some Fourteen Hundred Men blown together from all winds, on the deepest errand.

　　Yes, in that silent-marching mass there lies Futurity enough. No symbolic Ark, like the old Hebrews, do these men bear: yet with them too is a Covenant; they too preside at a new Era in the History of Men. (*FR*, 1:134)

Alison effaces himself by avoiding direct address of the reader (which implies a first-person addresser), by avoiding commentary on events, and by employing a plain style that seeks to efface writing itself. In order to avoid commentary, he imputes judgments to others (for example, to "the reflecting" who observe the preservation of feudal social distinctions). As narrator, he has no spatial relationship to the scene—

he seems to be nowhere—whereas Carlyle situates himself and his readers in the midst of the crowd watching the procession. Carlyle begins by exhorting the reader, in an exclamatory apostrophe—"Behold, however!"—to observe the scene he is describing. The second paragraph of the passage from *The French Revolution* (of which I have included only one-quarter) consists entirely of the narrator's commentary on the meaning of the event and contains no narrative of the event itself.[43] Throughout the passage, Carlyle's language draws attention to itself through the use of such rhetorical and literary devices as apostrophe, repetition and variation, alliteration, metaphor, and allusion (note the "Grecian birds" and the Ark of the Covenant). Most importantly, Carlyle devotes a whole chapter to this episode because of its symbolic importance—for him it foreshadows the whole course of the revolution—while Alison gives only one paragraph to a ceremony that, for him, has little significance in the chain of political events.

Carlyle's use of present-tense narration collapses the distance between past and present, emphasizing that meaning is not fixed in the past but is always in the process of being made. In a narrative that treats events as if they were taking place before the narrator's and reader's eyes, past and present are not separate, since the beliefs and actions that had constituted the revolution also constitute the lives of the narrator and his readers. Further, Carlyle dramatizes the revolution as it lives on in the present in moments when the time of narration—the moment of writing—converges with the time of historical events. When, for example, he writes of d'Artois that he "now, as a grey timeworn man, sits desolate at Grätz" and informs us in a footnote that "now" means "A.D. 1834," the year in which he is writing the passage, he abruptly brings the historical actor from the past into the present (1:33). The "now" of this passage is itself ever-shifting; the footnotes accompanying similar passages always indicate the moment at which he writes, at least one such note appearing for each of the three years (1834, 1835, 1836) during which he worked on the history (1:224, 3:47, 312).

The first-person plural (for example, "Our commons" in the quotation above) also telescopes the distance between past and present, narrator and narrated (see Vanden Bossche, "Revolution and Authority," 284–85; J. Rosenberg, 77–78). In the following passage, the referent of the word *we* shifts as the narrator comments on Danton's defense of the September massacres:

When applied to by an offical person, about the Orléans Prisoners, and the risks they ran, [Danton] answered gloomily, twice over, 'Are not these men guilty?'—When pressed, he 'answered in a terrible voice,' and turned his back. Two Thousand slain in the prisons; horrible if you will: but Brunswick is within a day's journey of *us;* and there are Five-and-twenty Millions yet, to slay or save. Some men have tasks,—frightfuller than *ours!* It seems strange, but is not strange, that this Minister of Moloch-Justice, when any suppliant for a friend's life got access to him, was found to have human compassion. (3:47; emphasis added)

The first-person plural ("us") in the third sentence (beginning "Two Thousand slain . . .") refers to Danton. Because there are no quotation marks to set Danton's speech off from the historical narrative (as in the first sentence), however, the speech merges with the narration, the narrated with the narrator. This elision continues in the concluding sentences, as the principal location of the speaking voice slides from Danton and the past to Carlyle and the present, the final sentence belonging only to the latter. The sentence that comes between ("Some men have . . .") may be attributed to either man and thus further merges them. If we read it together with the previous sentence, it becomes a continuation of Danton's speech, "ours" referring to the patriots who speak in the first person in that sentence. But if we read it together with the final sentence, it becomes part of Carlyle's commentary, suggesting that the "task" of the patriots in 1792 was more frightful than "ours" in the 1830s.

Carlyle also employs this technique to represent the revolution as a multiplicity of speakers and points of view. By merging with the historical actors, he is able to sympathize with each of them and to speak in all of their voices. He represents history as the interaction of groups, as dialogues between personifications like "universal Patriotism" and the "Legislative." In the following passage, he uses dashes to indicate an exchange of speeches between Parisian patriots and the revolutionary authorities:

Twelve Hundred slain Patriots, do they not, from their dark catacombs there, in Death's dumb-show, plead (O ye Legislators) for vengeance? . . . Nay, apart from vengeance, and with an eye to Public Salvation only, are there not still, in this Paris (in round numbers) "Thirty thousand Aristocrats," of the most malignant humour;

driven now to their last trump-card?—Be patient, ye Patriots: our
New High Court, "Tribunal of the Seventeenth," sits . . . and Danton, extinguishing improper judges, improper practices whereso-
ever found, is "the same man you have known at the Cordeliers."
With such a Minister of Justice, shall not Justice be done?—Let it be
swift, then, answers universal Patriotism; swift and sure!—(3:8–9)

While the quotations within the speeches assure us that the scene
is based on documentary evidence, the dialogue compresses a long
course of discussion and debate. These compressed dialogues seek to
represent, not the literal event, but its symbolic meaning. Because the
narrator merges with these voices rather than distinguishing them as
part of a past action, the text gives the impression that the narrator is
not the manipulator of the voices but the product of them. In *Sartor
Resartus*, the personae, who all sound like Carlyle, may be regarded as
avatars of the different aspects of his personality. In *The French Revolution*, he tries to get beyond the authorial ego in order to represent
the full range of historical figures (see Bakhtin, 299).[44]

The narrator of *The French Revolution*, a narrator who belongs to
the world he narrates, seeks to interpret this world by discovering
its symbols. He suggests, in a chapter entitled "Symbolic," that public events are "Symbolic Representation[s]" of belief (2:47). Whereas
Alison's narrative is organized in terms of the day-by-day chronology
of events, virtually every subdivision of Carlyle's history, which often
disregards chronology, focuses on the discovery of the symbolic import of events.[45] At every level of the narrative, titles refer to literal
events in which Carlyle discovers a symbolic import. The titles of the
three volumes of the history reveal its basic structure, the initial rebellion against the old imprisoning order ("The Bastille"), the attempt
to author a new social order ("The Constitution"), and the descent
into complete destruction ("The Guillotine"). The same is true for the
other subdivisions of the history; for example, the storming of the Bastille represents the determination of the French people to break down
the old social structure; "Viaticum" represents not only the death of
Louis XV but the last rites of monarchy; "The Paper Age," not just
the proliferation of printed matter but the ephemerality of its paper
productions; and "Dishonoured Bills," not just the depletion of the
treasury but the figurative bankruptcy of the old order. Carlyle's depiction of the royal family's unsuccessful attempt to flee France is almost
allegorical. The royal family flees in an overburdened and oversized

berline that consequently moves so slowly—indeed, Carlyle exaggerated its slowness—that it can be captured by a handful of peasants and retired dragoons.[46] Carlyle finds in the berline a symbol of the accretions of privilege and meaningless tradition with which monarchy had become encrusted and which made its downfall inevitable. Symbols of power, they in fact have made the monarch powerless and given the upper hand to the people.

In addition to discovering the symbolic import of individual events, Carlyle creates ironic contrasts through juxtaposition, often discovering that the symbolic import of one event undermines the intended symbolic message of another. The French intend the Feast of Pikes to express their belief in the principle of fraternity. But Carlyle is suspicious of such "theatrical" displays, contrasting them unfavorably with the ritual oaths they imitate, such as the Puritan "Solemn League and Covenant" and the "Hebrew Feast of Tabernacles," in which "A whole Nation gathered, in the name of the Highest" (2:47, 42). More significantly, however, the narrative that ensues in the following section, which represents a mutiny in the army, reveals that a violent feast of "pikes" will lead to anarchy, not fraternity. Similarly, Carlyle plays on the idiomatic and literal meanings of the French verb *marcher* ("to be in working order," but literally "to march") in order to contrast the failure of the constitution with the success of the troops from Marseilles. While "believing Patriots" think "that the Constitution will march, *marcher*,—had it once legs to stand on," Carlyle ironically contrasts their enfeebled constitution, which grows "rheumatic," "stagger[s]" and finally "will not march," with the vigorous Marseillais and their cry of "Let Us March" that brings about the insurrection of August 1792 (2:5, 223, 237; see 227).

If an epic represents the belief of a people as manifested in its actions, then the French Revolution, which manifested a nation's unbelief, provides problematic material for epic. Within his epic framework, Carlyle represents the actions of the French people as mockepic. The French need a deus ex machina (Carlyle's use of the English equivalent of this phrase, "god from the machine," already tends to deflate it) but get only an ineffectual "Mars de Broglie" and a royal usher "Mercury . . . de Brézé" (1:160). The epic machinery that motivates the action of the history becomes mere "preternatural suspicion" (1:126–27). Homer's "wine-dark sea" gets adapted as the mockheroic epithet "sea-green" to describe Robespierre. Finally, Carlyle

echoes "The Rape of the Lock" in his depiction of the queen preparing to flee as an epic heroine outfitting her hero: "New Clothes
are needed; as usual, in all Epic transactions, were it in the grimmest
iron ages; consider 'Queen Chrimhilde, with her sixty sempstresses,'
in that iron *Nibelungen Song*! No queen can stir without new clothes"
(2:157). Unlike Chrimhilde, who married the indomitable Siegfried
and wreaked terrible revenge on the enemies who killed him, however,
Marie Antoinette, married to the ineffectual Louis XVI, is absurdly
concerned with "perfumes" and "toilette-implements" that burden the
cumbersome "Argosy" in which the royal family insists on traveling
(2:157, 168; see *CME*, 2:238). Whereas Homer had been able to "sing"
the belief of a society in an epic poem, Carlyle can only express unbelief through "prose." Echoing the traditional epic invocation, he
writes: "The 'destructive wrath' of Sansculottism: this is what we *speak*,
having unhappily no voice for *singing*" (1:212; emphasis added). In a
work that persistently satirizes speech-making, it is particularly ironic
that his epic must be spoken.[47]

Just as *The French Revolution*'s epic aspirations are undermined by
mock-epic elements, so its overt narrative structure, which represents a
circular movement from the institution of monarchical order through
a period of transition following its destruction and concluding in the
constitution of democratic order, is undermined by a parallel narrative
that represents an uninterrupted current of accelerating destruction
and anarchy. The former narrative represents the desire to recover
authority while the latter suggests that the revolution can do nothing
but destroy it.

Both narratives share the same starting point in volume 1, the destruction of the monarchy as symbolized by "The Bastille." Carlyle
represents the bankrupt authority of the monarchy through the inability of successive finance ministers to avert financial default. Emp-
tied of authority, the institution of monarchy produces a king who can
no longer create social order. Although initially Louis compels obedience—he attempts to govern by royal edict—he cannot compel belief.
This situation cannot last long, and, with the storming of the Bastille,
power begins to shift to the people.

With volume 2, "The Constitution," the two narratives diverge, the
one representing the National Assembly's attempt to author a constitution and the other the increasing anarchy that undermines this
enterprise. An "incipient New Order of Society" appears to emerge

when the French express their beliefs through the grand ritual oath of allegiance celebrated in "The Feast of Pikes" (2:34). But the royalist mutiny in the army at Nanci exposes the absence of loyalty, the "unsightly *wrong-side* of that thrice glorious Feast of Pikes" (2:100). With the destruction of royal authority, no single authority can establish itself, and the army, which is "the very implement of rule and restraint, whereby all the rest was managed and held in order," becomes "precisely the frightfullest immeasurable implement of misrule" (2:73). In September 1791, the assembly completes a constitution intended to produce a new social order. But the constitutional monarchy that gives the king the power to veto all legislation only institutionalizes the conflict between the monarchy and the middle class. Louis attempts to assert his authority by vetoing all legislation, and, because authority is now fragmented, neither Louis nor the assembly can govern. Anarchy increases and overwhelms the assembly's attempts to establish order, and, on August 10, 1792, a new uprising overturns the constitutional monarchy. Just as the storming of the Bastille had overturned the old regime, so the insurrection of the tenth of August overturns the constitutional monarchy. Instead of discovering authority, the constitution has further undermined it.

In the final volume of the history, "The Guillotine," the attempt to author a second constitution becomes completely submerged in the growing anarchy of the Terror. Having discovered that authority could not be divided between the monarchy and the people, the assembly proceeds to abolish the institution of monarchy itself. "Regicide" completes the abolition of authority that began with the storming of the Bastille: "a King himself, or say rather Kinghood in his person, is to expire here" (3:107). However, when the people assume the authority formerly held by monarchy, they fail to establish social order and anarchy engulfs the nation.

Rebuilding the Social Structure

Carlyle represents the revolution as burning down the old social structure and attempting to build a new one by writing a constitution. *Sartor Resartus* had already employed the metaphor of masonry to represent the process of writing. The Editor of *Sartor* depicts himself as a bridge-builder spanning the sea that separates British readers from the German clothes philosopher. As in "The Reminiscence of James Carlyle," the bridge-maker connects heaven and earth; he is the pontiff and the Prometheus who "can bring new fire from Heaven" (225). As translator of Teufelsdröckh's philosophy, the Editor transmits the authority of German transcendentalism to the land of British empiricism. Or, to put it another way, he builds a bridge that enables us to pass from ordinary existence into the "promised land" (255).

But the Editor's metaphors ultimately suggest that his bridge leads us into an infernal chaos, not a transcendental idyll. He compares it, not to a bridge like Tieck's that leads to a land of faery, but to the bridge between hell and earth built by Sin and Death in *Paradise Lost* (79). Furthermore, he can only "conclude" but "not complete" it: "No firm arch, over-spanning the Impassible with paved Highway, could the Editor construct; only, as was said, some zigzag series of rafts floating tumultuously thereon" (268). Since this bridge is the Editor's metaphor for his project of transmitting in writing the life and opinions of Teufelsdröckh, that project appears to be a failure. As the Editor fails in his attempt to build a bridge to heaven, instead building one to hell, so the French fail to "build" a utopian social structure and instead create the Terror.

In Carlyle's history, the Bastille is *the* building, a metaphor for the entire social edifice of the *ancien regime*. Bastille is the generic name for a fortress, derived from the verb *bâtir*, to build: "they name [it] *Bastille, or Building,* as if there were no other building" (1:131). Carlyle calls the Bastille, along with other medieval buildings, a "realised ideal"; it is an expression of the feudal social order and of the structures of belief in which the nation resides. He further contends that, while the kings of France have passed away, the physical and social structures they "realised" remain, and names among these "realised ideals" both "Cathedrals" and a "Creed (or memory of a creed) in them," both "Palaces, and a State and Law" (1:8).

The metaphor of the social order as a house or building was already well established in political writing when Carlyle wrote *The French Revolution* (see Arac, *Commissioned Spirits*, 124). Burke uses it throughout his *Reflections on the Revolution*, arguing that although the old order suffered "waste and dilapidation," it still possessed "the foundations of a noble and venerable castle" that might have been "repaired" (40; see 24, 40, 56, 66, 79, 99, 105, 196–97). Carlyle takes up the same metaphor, but he treats it differently, finding that the social structure that had once served as a home—a protective "castle" as in "The Reminiscence of James Carlyle"—had become a prison, a Bastille. In fact, the Bastille had been built during the feudal era to protect the people of Paris from invasion, but by the eighteenth century, it was used only to imprison them and to suppress popular disturbances. The only solution is to destroy it and rebuild the social order.

Carlyle emphasizes that beliefs, not physical force, create and destroy these social structures. The destruction of the Bastille only symbolically enacts the destruction of "Old Feudal France" by *philosophes* like Voltaire and Diderot (*FR*, 2:201). In "Diderot," Carlyle describes the "End of a Social System . . . which for above a thousand years had been building itself together" as the destruction of a building, clearly the Bastille:

> active hands drive in their wedges, set to their crowbars; there is a comfortable appearance of work going on. Instead of here and there a stone falling out, here and there a handful of dust, whole masses tumble down, whole clouds and whirlwinds of dust: torches too are applied, and the rotten easily takes fire: so, what with flame-whirlwind, what with dust-whirlwind, and the crash of falling towers, the concern grows eminently interesting; and our assiduous craftsmen can encourage one another with *Vivats,* and cries of *Speed the work.* (*CME*, 3:179–80)

Carlyle interprets the attack on the Bastille as an attempt to destroy the old social order, the blows of the axes on the drawbridge aimed at "Tyranny" and its "whole accursed Edifice" (*FR*, 1:190). He deemphasizes the role of physical force by noting that only one Parisian died in the storming and concluding that the Bastille, "like the City of Jericho, was overturned by miraculous *sound,*" a reversal of the Orphic music that built Thebes (1:210; see *SR*, 263).

Carlyle's concern is that the processes of destruction, once unleashed, are difficult to control. Revolution, he writes, is: "the open violent Rebellion, and Victory, of disimprisoned Anarchy against corrupt worn-out Authority; how Anarchy breaks prison; bursts up from the infinite Deep, and rages uncontrollable, immeasurable, enveloping a world; in phasis after phasis of fever-frenzy;—till the frenzy burning itself out and what elements of new Order it held (since all Force holds such) developing themselves, the Uncontrollable be got, if not reimprisoned, yet harnessed, and its mad forces made to work towards their object as sane regulated ones" (1:211–12).[48] Fire is the most common and prominent metaphor in *The French Revolution*, almost always representing the uncontrolled spread of destruction: "Feudalism is struck dead . . . by fire; say, by self-combustion . . . in visible material combustion, château after château mounts up; in spiritual invisible combustion, one authority after another" (1:231, 2:107; see 227). The problem for the revolutionaries is how to "re-imprison" this revolutionary force.[49] The title of the chapter in which this passage appears, "Make the Constitution," points toward the next phase of the revolution; the attempt to "build" a new social edifice will be the subject of volume 2, "The Constitution." In the conclusion of this chapter, Carlyle introduces an analogy between the attempt to author the constitution and the project of building a social structure with a comment that suggests the difficulties and failures that lie ahead: "A Constitution can be built, Constitutions enough *à la Sieyes*" (1:215).

While the cathedrals and fortresses of the old social order had been, like James Carlyle's houses, constructed of lasting stone, however, the constitution built to house the new social order is made of ephemeral paper. None of the three constitutions Sieyes sets out to "build" lasts as long as a year. The first is a mere house of cards, a "card-castle" with a "top-paper" instead of a "top-stone": the "Edifice of the Constitution" or the "Constitutional Fabric, built with . . . explosive Federation Oaths, and its top-stone brought out with dancing and variegated radiance, went to pieces, like frail crockery . . . in eleven short months" (1:215, 221, 2:195, 203–4).[50] The second constitution, raised on the unstable "rubbish and boulders" of the first, also suffers "frequent perilous downrushing of scaffolding and rubble-work" and never even goes into effect (3:69). It is the quintessential paper constitution: "Further than *paper* it never got, nor ever will get" (3:186; emphasis added). The final constitution is just as fragile as its predecessors; it is another "paper-fabric" constructed by the hitherto unsuccessful "Architect," Sieyes. It only brings the process of writing constitutions to an end because it formalizes the social order that Napoleon imposes by force rather than providing a system of belief.

The metaphor of the paper building is an extension of Carlyle's representation of the eighteenth century as "The Paper Age," an era of "Book-paper, splendid with Theories, Philosophies, Sensibilities" (1:29). The *philosophes* have opened a "Pandora's box" of "printed paper": "street ballads," "epigrams," "Manuscript Newspapers," "pamphlets," and novels like "Saint-Pierre's *Paul et Virginie*, and Louvet's *Chevalier de Faublas*" (1:59, 55, 56, 60). After the storming of the Bastille, the proliferation of paper accelerates: "Committees of the Constitution, of Reports, of Researches . . . yield mountains of Printed Paper"; "Twelve Hundred pamphleteers" drone forth "perpetual pamphlets"; and "Placard Journal[s]" make their appeal to the penniless who cannot afford newspapers (1:219, 222, 28). The same inflationary process forces the government to pay its debts with devalued "Bank-paper," "Dishonoured Bills" (1:29; see 109).[51]

These metaphors interact in two ways to develop Carlyle's argument about the failure to author a constitution. First, the French build their constitutions out of combustible material vulnerable to the fires with which they have destroyed the old order. Since a paper constitution cannot adequately confine the forces that overturned the old social order, it is not "worth much more than the waste-paper it is written on" (1:215). Second, the revolutionaries fail to transform the fire with which they have destroyed the old order into a creative tool for producing a permanent and substantial social order. They cannot find a "Prometheus" who bears, not the fire of destruction, but a divine spark that can "draw thunder and lightning out of Heaven to sanction" the Constitution (2:5, 1:215; see 2:64). Like Burke, Carlyle fears that the revolutionaries can only destroy, that their fire will produce only a "fire-consummation," not a "fire-creation" (*FR*, 1:213; see 3:297–98; *SR*, 244; *Reflections*, 79). Instead of building a heavenly city that recuperates paradise, they build a Tower of Babel—or, in a variant of this figure, "an overturned pyramid, on its vertex"—that produces only social fragmentation (*FR*, 2:189, 195, 198).[52]

Carlyle's history argues that a written document cannot produce social order unless it reflects the very structure of national life: "The Constitution, the set of Laws, or prescribed Habits of Acting, that men will live under, is the one which images their Convictions,—their Faith as to this wondrous Universe." It is not enough to build a constitutional structure, Carlyle adds, you must build it so that people will "come and live in" it (1:215). The idea that a written document could be used to articulate a body of fundamental principles through which a state is constituted was a new one. The "British constitution" was a set of principles established by tradition and precedent, not a written document like the constitutions of the United States and France. While the unwritten constitution corresponds to the oral tra-

dition of Homer and the Bible, Carlyle treats the written constitution
as he does self-conscious epic. Like the oral epic, the unwritten constitution is unself-conscious and therefore authoritative. Carlyle makes
this distinction explicit in an early chapter of *The French Revolution*:
"Herein too, in this its System of Habits, acquired, retained how you
will, lies the true Law-Code and Constitution of a Society; the only
Code, though an unwritten one, which it can in nowise *dis*obey. The
thing we call written Code, Constitution, Form of Government, and
the like, what is it but some miniature image, and solemnly expressed
summary of this unwritten Code? *Is,*—or rather, alas, is *not;* but only
should be, and always tends to be!" (1:38).[53] Without divine sanction,
the legislative cannot produce a constitution that corresponds to the
constitution that already exists unconsciously; its constitution corresponds only to theories that serve particular interest groups, not the
nation as a whole (see 1:219). The paper constitution represents the
historicity of all writing, and therefore its inability, in Carlyle's view,
to provide the foundation for social order.

Authoring the Constitution: The Problem of Closure

The French Revolution posits the problem of how to "reimprison" or reenclose anarchy once it has been "disimprisoned." "Closure" has two
conventional senses. First, it refers to the way in which a narrative is
given a sense of ending, of completion. Second, it refers to the aim
of a text to enclose its meaning, its aspiration to be a complete and
total representation. Both kinds of closure may be regarded as illusory, but this has never prevented authors from seeking to achieve it
(see Barthes, "Work to Text"; Derrida; D. Miller; Lotman, 232–39;
Vanden Bossche, "Desire and Deferral of Closure"). Carlyle's texts
dramatize both the desire for closure and the difficulty of achieving it.
Sartor Resartus, "Characteristics," and *The French Revolution* each represents an attempt to achieve closure by creating a totalizing text, as
mythus, philosophy of life, or constitution. Carlyle's later explorations
of the problem of closure in "Characteristics" and *The French Revolution*
question the optimism with which he had imagined Teufelsdröckh's
achievement of closure when he set out to write a new mythus, and
shed light on Carlyle's own effort to create a totalizing epic.

"Characteristics" (1831), the first essay Carlyle wrote after completing *Sartor Resartus*, took shape after he suggested to the editor of the *Edinburgh Review* that several recent books—Thomas Hope's *An Essay on the Origin and Prospects of Man* (1831), Friedrich Schlegel's *Philosophische Vorlesungen* (1830), William Godwin's *Thoughts on Man* (1831), and a new work by Coleridge, probably *Aids to Reflection* (1831)— were attempts to create totalizing philosophies of life, the equivalent of the *Palingenesia* that Teufelsdröckh was supposed to be writing at that moment (*CL*, 6:13). The essay transposes Teufelsdröckh's development into a representation of the development of contemporary society and examines the writings of Hope and Schlegel as products of that development. Like Teufelsdröckh, society has lost the freedom of its idyllic youth and is now locked away in a "prison-house of the soul" (*CME*, 3:2); both become wanderers, suffering the "fever of Scepticism," the "fever-paroxysms of Doubt" (*CME*, 3:40; *SR*, 114); society is crushed by "the Juggernaut wheels" of a "dead mechanical idol" just as Teufelsdröckh encounters a "huge, dead, immeasurable Steam-engine, rolling on, in its dead indifference, to grind [him] limb from limb" (*CME*, 3:29; *SR*, 164); Teufelsdröckh is caught in the Centre of Indifference between the Everlasting No and the Everlasting Yea, and the current era has "dared to say No and cannot yet say Yea" (*CME*, 3:31); having completed the process of destroying "worn-out Symbols," it must, like Teufelsdröckh, begin to "construct" new ones, to author a new Genesis (*CME*, 3:31, 33; see 26ff.).

While Carlyle discovers signs that society has begun to create new mythuses, he does not ultimately find much hope for Teufelsdröckh's project in the totalizing schemes of Hope and Schlegel. At first, he thinks that there are some hopeful signs: German literature is taking over the functions of religion; the English Utilitarians—he undoubtedly has J. S. Mill in mind—are looking beyond the limits of Utilitarianism; and the French appear to be turning from destruction to the creation of a new religion—a clear reference to the St. Simonians (*CME*, 3:40–42). But when Carlyle examines the writings of Hope and Schlegel, he discovers that they are products of the era of revolutionary change rather than means of enabling it to achieve transcendental closure. His description of Hope's book as a "painful, confused stammering, and struggling" that "maunders, low, long-winded . . . in . . . endless convolutions" anticipates his description of Cagliostro's Babelian discourse (*CME*, 3:34). Like Teufelsdröckh and Cagliostro, Hope speaks in confused "circumvolutions," opening up an "endless" discourse that reinforces revolution rather than achieving closure (*CME*, 3:293; see *SR*, 31). Although Carlyle has greater hopes for Schlegel's "clear . . . precise and vivid" language, he, too, fails to achieve closure, his lectures literally ending in mid-sentence "with an 'Aber——,' with a 'But——'!" (*CME*, 3:34, 35). Carlyle concludes that any philosophy or "theorem of the world" that claims to provide a totalizing representation but lacks transcendental authority will be "found wanting"; after all, he concludes, "what Theorem of the Infinite can the Finite render complete?" (*CME*, 3:6, 25; see 38). Writing only produces more writing; it does not achieve closure.

The French Revolution explores the problem of closure in two writing projects that echo two similar projects in *Sartor Resartus*. The revolutionaries' project of writing the constitution in *The French Revolution* repeats and revises both the Editor's project of writing the life and opinions of Diogenes Teufelsdröckh and Teufelsdröckh's project of writing the *Clothes Volume* and the *Palingenesia*. *Sartor Resartus* problematizes the possibility of closure but holds open the possibility that closure can be achieved, while *The French Revolution* undermines the possibilities that *Sartor Resartus* offers. All of the projects in turn reflect on Carlyle's (or his narrator's) project of writing an epic history of the revolution.

The narratives of Teufelsdröckh's life and of the French Revolution run parallel courses, and both have problematic closures. Teufelsdröckh becomes a prisoner of time and eighteenth-century mechanistic philosophy; the French people are prisoners of outworn feudal monarchy. The "sansculotte" Diogenes Teufelsdröckh "breaks-off his neck-halter"; the French people "break prison." After they destroy the old social structures, both Teufelsdröckh and the French people find themselves without any fixed points of reference, without access to transcendental authority. Like sailors with no "Loadstar," both must wander aimlessly, and endlessly (*SR*, 154; see Landow, "Swim or Drown," *Images of Crisis*, 59–63).

The Editor of *Sartor* and the French legislature both attempt to use writing to produce closure, defining a moment when authority is recovered and the new social order inaugurated. For the Editor of *Sartor*, this moment comes when Teufelsdröckh decides to author a new mythus, and for the French legislature when they author their constitution. Both depict this as a moment that brings wandering to an end; Teufelsdröckh reaches a celestial summit and the French reach "harbor." It also brings the endless motion of revolution to a close; the Editor of *Sartor* declares that Teufelsdröckh's character is now fixed and "no new revolution . . . is to be looked for," and the constituent assembly concludes that "the glorious . . . Revolution is complete" (*SR*, 204; *FR*, 2:197).

In their quest for closure, however, the revolutionaries have proceeded a step further than Teufelsdröckh, actually writing the constitution whereas Teufelsdröckh has not yet begun to author his new mythus, but this constitution merely reveals the shortcomings of all totalizing texts. The fact that these moments of closure occur only about two-thirds of the way through each work, well before the narrative itself is complete, suggests that they will be problematic. In *Sartor Resartus*, closure at this point does not at first appear to be problematic because it coincides with the end of the biographical narrative that constitutes book 2. But when the analogous moment of closure arrives in *The French Revolution*, the narrative is far from complete. Whereas the Editor of *Sartor Resartus* validates Teufelsdröckh's moment of closure, the narrator of *The French Revolution* challenges the legislative's claim that it has ended the revolution: "The Revolution is finished, then? . . . Your Revolution, like jelly sufficiently *boiled*, needs only to be poured into *shapes*, of Constitution, and 'consolidated' therein?" (1:234). The narrator's doubts are soon confirmed when the constitution "bursts in pieces." A closer examination of *Sartor Resartus* will reveal that it too questions, though less directly, the Editor's discovery of closure.

In order to comprehend the nature of closure in these texts, we must examine them structurally as well as thematically. Carlyle could not reconcile himself to the narrative structure he found in the writings of Goethe, the structure dictated by *bildung*.[54] In these narratives, each adventure that moves the exiled hero farther away from home also brings him or her one step closer to it, but the home to which the hero returns is not exactly the same place from which he or she departed because the hero has been changed by the process of the journey. Carlyle attempts to escape this dialectic by keeping its terms oppositional rather than letting them be synthesized in the return home. Because he cannot regard a step away from home as a step back toward it, his heroes move steadily away from home until they suddenly find themselves back again. The home is exactly the same as the one they left behind because it is a perfect idyll that cannot be improved. Yet because heroes are fallen and exiled, they can never be certain that the home regained really is the same as the home lost. Whereas the hero of *bildung* seems to move upward in a rising spiral, Carlyle's heroes, unable to escape history, travel in an endless circle. Nimmo studies endlessly; Werner, and even Schiller, wander endlessly; Coleridge and Dalbrook speak endlessly; but none of them gets anywhere. Of all the moderns, only Goethe is able to return to his "inward home" and achieve rest, and Carlyle eventually came to doubt even this achievement.

The fundamental structure of *Sartor Resartus* is endless circling. Teufelsdröckh's final words, "*Es geht an* (It is beginning)," in addition to evoking the revolutionary *Ça ira,* suggest that, at the very end of the narrative, the privileged moment of closure, he is embarking once again on a quest for authority. Similarly, the Everlasting Yea turns out to be a beginning—the beginning absent from the opening of the biographical section of *Sartor,* rather than a moment of closure. Although the Editor entitles the first chapter of book 2 "Genesis" in order to stress origins and beginnings, he concedes that Teufelsdröckh's first appearance on earth is an "Exodus" (81). Teufelsdröckh's Genesis, or beginning, occurs instead at the conclusion of the biographical narrative when he is reborn as an author who exclaims, "Let there be Light!" (197). Even the Everlasting Yea is undercut. Borrowing the traditional imagery of closure from spiritual autobiography, the Editor dramatically concludes the biographical section of *Sartor Resartus* with Teufelsdröckh ascending "the higher sunlight slopes . . . of that Mountain which has no summit, or whose summit is in heaven only" (184; see Peterson, 39). But the framing sections of *Sartor Resartus,* books 1 and 3, comically deflate this closure. Book 1 reduces the sublime summit to the comically finite heights of the "highest house in the Wahngasse" while also transferring it from the celestial realms to urban Weissnichtwo. In the final chapter of book 3, Teufelsdröckh abandons even this "watchtower." In spite of the Editor's earlier assertion that "no new revolution" is to be anticipated in Teufelsdröckh's life, Teufelsdröckh has reportedly fomented a sedition of tailors and appears to be journeying toward Paris at the moment of the July Revolution.

One might suppose that Teufelsdröckh is more successful at achieving closure than the Editor of *Sartor Resartus* is at representing it. Certainly, Carlyle projects his own desire for a totalizing myth into his characterization of Teufelsdröckh's project. The fate of Teufelsdröckh's *Palingenesia*, however, seems to be written in the fate of totalizing texts, like the philosophies of Hope and Schlegel and the French constitutions, that Carlyle represented in later works. In *Sartor Resartus* itself, we are left doubting whether the *Palingenesia* can ever be written. Some readers have argued that *Sartor* itself is the *Palingenesia*, but it is useful to insist on *Sartor*'s fiction that *Die Kleider, ihr Werden und Wirken* (Clothes, their Origin and Influence) is only Teufelsdröckh's first step toward producing a new cultural mythus. *Die Kleider*, he tells us, is preliminary to the "Transcendent or ultimate portion" of his work, and the *Palingenesia* remains unpublished, perhaps unfinished, when Teufelsdröckh disappears at the end of *Sartor Resartus* (199, 217, 297). *Die Kleider* only brings him to the end of a historical cycle; rebirth will not begin until he publishes the *Palingenesia*. Since Carlyle turned away from speculative philosophy after *Sartor Resartus*, this mythus for the new era could not take the form imagined in *Sartor*. It must turn to fact and history; the rebirth of society will not be represented in the *Palingenesia* but in *The French Revolution*.

In *The French Revolution*, the French, like Teufelsdröckh, seek to achieve closure but circle endlessly without getting anywhere. The three volumes of the history all offer and then undercut a moment of closure. This structural circling, further reinforced by the pervasive imagery of circling, puts into question not only the possibility that the French can create a new social order but that writing can ever achieve closure.

In the first volume of *The French Revolution*, the legislative intends to conclude the revolution by writing a constitution, but the process of authoring it extends rather than concludes the revolution. The revolution again appears to come to an end at the climax of volume 2, when the king accepts the constitution, but at the conclusion of this volume, the constitution bursts in pieces. Although volume 3 brings the history to a close, its closure does not resolve the problems raised in the first two volumes. By rapidly repeating a sequence of events parallel to those in volumes 1 and 2, it suggests that, instead of achieving closure, the revolution is accelerating toward total destruction. The final volume begins with a book entitled "September" (in reference to the September massacres) and circles round to conclude with "Vendémiaire," the month that corresponds to September in the revolutionary calendar. Both represent France in an autumnal state, trapped in the endless movement toward wintry death that is never completed, never brought fully round to the season of rebirth. The conclusion of the history, a fictitious *ex post facto* prophecy, predicts the course of the revolution that has been the subject of Carlyle's history, thus circling us back through the history of the revolution, just as the narrator circles endlessly between the historical moment in which he is writing and the historical moment he records.

While the aim of authoring the constitution is to enable the French people to escape revolution and history, the final volume insists that the revolution continues, that "the end is not yet" (3:314). The end of the Terror does not end revolution but is itself a "new glorious Revolution"; only the "body of Sansculottism" dies, its soul "still lives, and is not dead, but changed . . . still works far and wide, through one bodily shape into another less amorphous" (3:286, 310–11). Just as Teufelsdröckh's disappearance at the end of *Sartor Resartus* leaves him once again wandering Europe—is he in Paris, is he in London?—the French fail to achieve the repose of closure, the "blind brute Force" of the revolution offering "no rest . . . but in the grave" (3:249). At the conclusion of the history, the French have not returned to the prerevolutionary idyll, but have circled back to the moment at which the old order disintegrated. In 1795, Napoleon's "whiff of grapeshot" gratuitously succeeds where Broglie's had failed in 1789; the French people are still demanding "bread, not bursts of Parliamentary eloquence"; and France is still ruled by the "Aristocracy," albeit an "Aristocracy of the Moneybag" rather than an "Aristocracy of Feudal Parchment" (3:303, 320). The topos of impossible closure is reinforced throughout *The French Revolution* by the imagery of endless circling. It should not be surprising that the revolution—the word *revolution* itself originally denoted the circular orbit of celestial bodies, and then the general notion of cyclical periodicity—spreads in ever-widening circles. Whirlpools of Society, whirlpools of Babylonish confusion, regurgitating whirlpools of men and women, World-Whirlpools, whirlblasts, waste vortices, red blazing whirlwinds, fire-whirlwinds, clashing whirlwinds, whirlwinds of military fire and of human passions, and tornados of fatalism "spin" through the pages of the history (1:65, 2:121, 192, 1:169, 2:151, 1:219, 2:299, 222, 3:151, 2:170, 3:70, 122, 212). If the narrative spirals, it spirals downward, not upward; but, most importantly, it spirals without end, descending into "endless Conflagration[s]" and "bottomless cataracts" (2:152, 251).

In *Sartor Resartus*, Carlyle held out the hope that authors who work with words, like laborers who till the soil, could produce something outside themselves, could create a world (see 227–28). Yet Teufelsdröckh the author also believes that "Conviction, were it never so excellent, is worthless till it convert itself into Conduct. Nay, properly Conviction is not possible till then; inasmuch as all Speculation is by nature endless, formless, a vortex amid vortices" (195).[55] In "Characteristics," Carlyle complains that in this "age of Metaphysics" during which "the arena of free *Activity* has long been narrowing, that of sceptical Inquiry becoming more and more universal. . . . our best effort must be unproductively spent not in *working*, but in ascertaining our mere Whereabout, and so much as whether we are to *work* at all" (*CME*, 3:27–28; emphasis added). Since knowledge is never complete, action tends to be deferred endlessly.

In "Characteristics," Carlyle had condemned contemporary society for its reliance on metaphysical theory or speculation that remains locked in language and cannot be realized in action or social structures. Because society has fallen from the idyll of shared unconscious unity into Babelian fragmentation—"Religion split[ting] itself into Philosophies"—each individual is locked into a self-created universe of private belief in which language necessarily turns in upon itself (*CME*, 3:15, 33). This inward-turning tendency manifests itself as autophagy: "self-devouring" reviews feed off literature, and in turn a "Review of Reviews" feeds off other reviews (*CME*, 3:25). Carlyle brilliantly expresses Victorian anxiety about the autophagic tendency of self-conscious philosophy in the image of the Irish saint who carries his head in his mouth: "Consider it well, Metaphysics is the attempt of the mind to rise above the mind; to environ and shut in, or as we say, *comprehend* the mind. Hopeless struggle, for the wisest, as for the foolishest! What strength of sinew, or athletic skill, will enable the stoutest athlete to fold his own body in his arms, and, by lifting, lift up *himself*? The Irish Saint swam the Channel, 'carrying his head in his teeth;' but the feat has never been imitated" (*CME*, 3:27; see Hartman).

Because the attempt to establish belief through metaphysical speculation can never achieve closure, one can never stop speculating and begin acting. Anticipating the imagery of *The French Revolution*, Carlyle depicts speculation "circulat[ing] in endless vortices," "wander[ing] homeless" and declining into "endless realms of Denial" (*CME*, 3:27, 30, 26).[56] It is appropriate that he contemplated including Coleridge among the authors he might discuss in "Characteristics," for he had long associated the poet and philosopher with the treachery of speech and metaphysical speculation. The letters Carlyle wrote after his first meeting with Coleridge in 1824 describe him as grotesquely over-weight—one is reminded of the appetite of Cagliostro—and addicted to endless "*tawlk*" (*CL*, 3:228, 300). Unable to achieve closure—"He is without beginning or middle or end . . . speaks incessantly . . . there is no method in his talk; he wanders like a man sailing among many currents"—he cannot realize his aimless talk in writing, let alone in action (*CL*, 3:139, 91; see 90, 351–52). The philosopher Dalbrook in *Wotton Reinfred*, patterned on these portrayals of Coleridge, has the same tendency to make language circle back on itself until its endless self-reflections make it meaningless: "The whole day long, if you do not check him, he will pour forth floods of speech, and the richest, noblest speech, only that you find no purpose, tendency, or meaning in it!" (*WR*, 80). Like Coleridge, Dalbrook does not realize his speech in writing or action; although he "has the loftiest idea of what is to be done, he does and feels that he can do nothing" and so "only talks the more" (*WR*, 81).[57]

The French Revolution provides a similar critique of theoretical specu-lation. The French, too, have fragmented belief and authority. First, "Twelve Hundred Kings"—the legislative—replace the single mon-arch; then the entire nation replaces the legislative and "there is prop-erly no Constituted Authority, but every man is his own King" (2:35, 3:40; see 59). The execution of the king, which destroys the last ves-tige of hierarchical authority, is "the last act these men ever did with concert" (3:112). Instead of social order there is a "duel of Authority with Authority," "as many Parties as there are Opinions" (1:84, 3:116).

This collapse of authority leads once again to autophagic self-destruction. To Burke's lament that the "age of chivalry is gone," Car-lyle replies that the "Age of Hunger" has come (2:228, 263). Hunger represents the fundamental human needs that are no longer satisfied when the ethical system that ensures the just satisfaction of those needs collapses (see 1:130–31). While chivalry and theocracy had served that function, hunger, from Carlyle's point of view, is simply what remains when the ethical system breaks down. The principles of the *philoso-phes*, who believe in political economy, do not provide a satisfactory system of justice: "What bonds that ever held a human society hap-pily together, or held it together at all, are in force here?" Carlyle asks them; their only belief, he concludes, is "that Pleasure is pleasant. Hunger they have for all sweet things; and the law of Hunger: but what other law?" (1:36–37; see 31).

In the absence of any moral system, society reverts to "fact," its "lowest, least blessed fact" being "the primitive one of Cannibalism: That *I* can devour *Thee*" (1:55). Cannibalism, as Carlyle suggests, is social autophagy. Having killed off the royal father, the revolution-ary "brothers" swear a "fraternal oath," but without a father to keep order, they turn on one another, becoming a "Brotherhood of Cain" (3:263; see 256). When the revolutionaries send each other to the guillotine during the Terror, the revolution begins "devouring its own children" (3:201, 254). The connotations of devouring in the word *con-sume* give a special resonance to Carlyle's repeated description of the Terror as the apocalyptic "Consummation of Sansculottism" (3:202, 222, 236, 243). The imagery of cannibalism pervades the history: Foulon is beheaded and his mouth stuffed with grass after he suggests that the starving people eat grass (1:112); the guillotine devours its victims (1:56, 3:253); a "Thyestes" feast precipitates the insurrection of women (1:247–48); and the revolutionaries reportedly make wigs from the hair of executed women and leather from the skin of men (3:246–47; see also 2:70, 231, 241, 3:71, 205, 253–54; J. Rosenberg, 91–100; Sterrenburg, passim; Brantlinger, 69). Because the revolu-tion "has the property of growing by . . . Hunger," it consumes virtually every figure who plays a major role in it: Louis XVI and the royal family, Mirabeau, Danton, the leading Girondists, Marat, and Robes-pierre, who becomes the appropriate symbol of the revolutionary gov-ernment that "has to consume itself, suicidally" when he attempts suicide after his arrest (2:17, 3:71; see 3:174, 231, 254, 273).

As in "Cagliostro" and "Characteristics," cannibalistic hunger, which can never be satisfied because speech never achieves closure, represents the oral activity that annihilates the other by absorbing it to itself. Carlyle notes that the majority of the leaders of the revo-lution were "eloquent" lawyers "skilful in Advocate-fence" who, be-lieving that "Society might become *methodic,* demonstrable by logic," attempt to found a social system on the basis of theoretical speculation, but, as in "Characteristics," he objects that "all theories, were they never so earnest, painfully elaborated, are . . . incomplete" (3:123, 1:54; see 148–51). Their principles do not provide an ethical system like chivalry; hence their "constitution" does not provide "bread to eat," that is, a just distribution of basic goods (1:226). Instead, the legislative, preoccupied with "debating, denouncing, objurgating" and "bursts of parliamentary eloquence," can produce nothing outside of itself, must feed on and "devour *itself*" (2:237). Like Coleridge and Dalbrook, parliaments—literally places of speaking—are unsuited to action; sending "your fifty-thousandth part of a new Tongue-fencer into National Debating-club" or "National *Palaver*" will produce only "talk" (2:26, 198). For Carlyle, parliamentary or legislative "acts" are not true actions; they are only documents sealed off from the world of social activity. The *sansculottes* never establish their authority; their ideas never get beyond paper.

Although Carlyle is suspicious of theories, his history has its own implicit theory of why the revolution occurred, why it failed, and how its course might have been altered. Implicitly, he also seeks to demonstrate how to reestablish social order in the present. The revolution occurred because the monarchy had lost authority; it had broken down "after long rough tear and wear" (1:7). The existing aristocracy inaugurated the era of cannibalism and consumption; Louis XVI is, like his father, a "Donothing and Eatall" whose court contents itself with shooting "partridges and grouse" (1:12, 22).[58] But, while Carlyle therefore concludes that the French people were justified in overturning the government, he does not believe them capable of establishing a new social order.

The people have a kind of authority, but it is an inverse authority capable of producing only an "inverse order," an *"organised . . . Anarchy"* (3:231; see 3:4). While the overindulging aristocracy no longer understands basic human needs, the people, who understand hunger, are a "genuine outburst of Nature," even *"trans*cendental" (1:251, 3:2). The "creative Mountain" becomes a "great Authority" that can get the sansculottic nation "accoutred" again (3:123, 122, 180, 140; see 2:249). But Carlyle ultimately distinguishes this knowledge of human need from knowledge of how to justly satisfy human need. While both kinds of knowledge require that one look beyond the surface, an action that the existing aristocracy was incapable of performing, the *sansculottes* do not discover the transcendental, but the "dread foundations" and "subterranean deeps" of "Madness and Tophet" (3:2, 2:279, 3:1;

see 1:80, 2:279). Since the people would never be anything more than an anarchic mass, France needed a leader with transcendental authority.[59]

Although *The French Revolution* does not explicitly invoke the idea of hero-worship (which Carlyle had already introduced in *Sartor Resartus*), its epic framework enables it to suggest the unfulfilled alternative to popular authority and a paper constitution, the discovery of a hero who could create a new hierarchy. In 1789, he writes, the French aristocracy was "still a graduated Hierarchy of Authorities, or the accredited Similitude of such: they sat there, uniting King with Commonalty; transmitting and translating *gradually*, from degree to degree, the command of one into the Obedience of the other" (2:232). As opposed to *an-archy*—the absence of *arche* or rule—there had formerly been a *mon-arch*—a single ruler and "reverend Hierarchies" (1:9). Whereas *hier-archy*, holy-rule, transmits authority from the divinity to the people, now "One *reverend* thing after another ceases to meet *reverence* . . . one authority after another" (2:106–7; emphasis added; see 2:262, 3:3, 40). Carlyle seeks throughout his history a hero who could reestablish this hierarchy.

Carlyle attempts to represent Mirabeau, whom he compares throughout the history to Hercules, as a potential epic hero; but he fails to fill even this tenuous role. Carlyle argues that Mirabeau, the sole revolutionary to possess a transcendental "sacred spark," might have become "king" if he had lived another year (2:134). Although he is a "world-compeller" who turns aside from the endless convolutions of parliamentary debate in order to engage in concrete action, it is not at all clear that his attempt to save the monarchy by establishing it on a constitutional basis would have succeeded, even if he had lived. More importantly, Carlyle's representation of Mirabeau as a man who disdains words and theoretical systems in favor of action, based on the elder Mirabeau's assertion that his son has "made away with (*humé*, swallowed) all *Formulas*" turns out to be problematic (2:137, 1:125; see 137). Carlyle's translation of *humé* as "made away with" suggests that Mirabeau has discarded formulas and theories, but the more exact translation, cited in parentheses, suggests that he has gullibly accepted, or "swallowed," them. Mirabeau the swallower turns out to be another cannibalistic revolutionary rather than a creative hero. Unable to make Mirabeau an epic hero, Carlyle must relegate his history to the domain of "tragedy" (2:147; see Farrell, 215–31).

Napoleon comes closer to enacting the role of the hero as a man of action. Unlike the leaders who preceded him—Mirabeau, Danton, Robespierre—Napoleon does not serve in the legislative and is not a man of words. He is a man of action who uses physical force—sansculottism "drilled now into Soldiership"—to create the "first germ of returning Order for France" (3:297, 54). He ends the revolution, not by writing a constitution, but by subduing the insurrection of Vendémiaire with a "whiff of grapeshot." Whereas Mirabeau failed to restore monarchy, Napoleon becomes the modern "Citizen King" (3:322).

Yet whereas Mirabeau and Danton may have compelled belief— they "ken"—but were unable to compel obedience, Napoleon compels obedience—he "cans"—but cannot compel belief. Napoleon's actions produce order only in the sense that they impose a legal structure, military discipline; they do not realize a transcendental ideal or the belief of the French people. His failure to reclothe the society stripped naked by the *sansculottes* becomes manifest when women wearing "flesh-coloured drawers" beneath their sheer empire gowns make nakedness the latest fashion. The social order that emerges at the end of the history is not a new system of belief but a return to the injustices with which it originated, the new "Evangel of Mammon" replacing the aristocratic feudal order with a "baser sort of Aristocracy" that is no better than the "Evangel of Jean Jacques" (3:314–15). The revolution clears the ground for the hegemony of political economy, the concern of Carlyle's next major works, *Chartism* and *Past and Present*, in which, like the French people, he asks, "Can the human stomach satisfy itself with lectures on Free-trade?" (3:136).

The argument of *The French Revolution*, that all attempts to author a totalizing text in an era that has undermined authority will fail, ultimately applies to *The French Revolution* itself. The book is not an epic as Carlyle defined the genre in "On Biography" but demonstrates the impossibility of epic. Any pretense of closure would be false. Just as the Editor of *Sartor Resartus* could only "conclude if not complete" his narrative, so the narrator of *The French Revolution* acknowledges that his history "does not conclude, but merely ceases" (3:321). Throughout the history, Carlyle persistently questions his own ability to discover the meaning of a phenomenon that undermines all meaning. Indeed, he undermines closure in his conclusion by introducing, in spite of his insistence that he is producing factual history, a patent fiction spoken by a notorious liar, a prophecy by the "Archquack" Cagliostro

(3:322).[60] What makes *The French Revolution* great is precisely Carlyle's openness to the heterogeneity of the history he was recording and the brilliantly heterogeneous vehicle he created to represent it. His history radically reshaped epic, but he sought in epic something other than what he created in *The French Revolution*: he sought a text that would reenclose the forces set loose by the revolution and dazzlingly represented in his history of it.

While *The French Revolution* seems to teach the lesson that one must stop talking and begin to act, Carlyle clearly prefers men of words like Mirabeau and Danton to men of action like Napoleon. Nor did he give up words himself. Instead, he tried to use writing to get to the end of writing. A typical pattern began to emerge in his letters and journals. While he was working on a project, he would long to finish writing so that he could return home to Scotland and rest, demonstrating his longing for closure and an affirmation that writing can achieve it. But the closures Carlyle achieved through writing never satisfied him for long. No sooner had he completed a project and made his way to Scotland than he would begin to grow restless and feel the need to write again. In the works that followed, he sought a way out of this dilemma by searching for authority in the acts of political leaders rather than in the writings of poets—the poetic king rather than the legislating poet. Napoleon and Mirabeau did not finally fulfill his vision of the active hero—but another political leader might. Furthermore, Carlyle could no longer be satisfied with merely analyzing society; he must somehow seek to change it. His writings to this point had sought to *know* the forces that had created modern society; they would now attempt to *act* upon it.

FOUR

Authoring the Polity: 1838–1850

"THIS IS NOT so much a history, as an epic poem; and notwithstanding, or even in consequence of this, the truest of histories" (Seigel, 52). So began J. S. Mill's enthusiastic notice of *The French Revolution* just two months after its appearance in May of 1837. For the first time, a work appeared with the name "Thomas Carlyle" on the title page; he was now an author, an authority.[1] Mill's early notice set the tone for the enthusiastic reviews that followed, including those by Thackeray in the *Times*, Thomas Anstey in the *Dublin Review*, John Heraud in *Fraser's*, and John Forster in the *Examiner*; even reviewers who did not approve of *The French Revolution* acknowledged that Carlyle was someone to be reckoned with. By 1840, he had been discussed in all the major reviews—the *Edinburgh*, *Quarterly*, *London and Westminster*, and *Dublin Reviews*—the latter three publishing extensive, omnibus reviews of his collected works. With this success, his publishers rushed out new editions of *Sartor Resartus*, his collected essays, and his translation of *Wilhelm Meister*. Satisfied that the book was admired and confident that he had finally found an audience, Carlyle felt at last that he had been granted authority to speak (*CL*, 9:272; see 311, 316, 328, 335).

The elite of London society—"Ladies this and Ladies that . . . old men of four score; men middle-aged with fine steel-grey heads; young men of the Universities, of the Law professions"—now came to hear him lecture (*CL*, 10:94). He was introduced to leaders of the Whig aristocracy, including Lord and Lady Holland, Lord Morpeth, Lord and Lady Harriet Baring, as well as Thomas Spring Rice, the chancellor of the Exchequer (*CL*, 9:335, 10:28, 66, 11:19, 38, 40, 130, 12:80, 104; Kaplan, 257). He also made the rounds of London's intellectual and artistic circles, encountering the likes of Henry Hallam,

William Whewell, Alfred de Vigny, Charles Babbage, Daniel Webster, William Gladstone, William Charles Macready, Charles Dickens, Geraldine Jewsbury, and Alfred Tennyson. He was in demand not only as a guest at dinner parties, but as a supporter of public causes like the copyright bill, the penny post, and the founding of the London library (*CME*, 4:205–7; *CL*, 10:79–81; Christianson, "Universal Penny Postage"; Kaplan, 262–63). And now that he had succeeded in literature and no longer had need of them, the academic posts he had sought in vain were offered to him.

Having been granted authority, he wished to use it to author a new social order. *The French Revolution* had been an inverse epic—not the belief, but the unbelief—of his culture. He now sought to author an epic that expressed belief and would restore authority to English society. The theme of "past and present" that dominated his writings during this period was the natural outcome of his attempt to create an epic out of the history of the past that would function as the mythic expression of belief for the present. Throughout the next decade he returned again and again to Cromwell and the Puritan era, while at the same time he was persistently drawn to the problems of the present day. Out of this dual concern, he shaped a new genre of social criticism that found its finest expression, naturally enough, in *Past and Present*.

Carlyle responded to the severe economic hardships Britain suffered between 1838 and 1850 with his most important works of social criticism. The first of the series of economic recessions that were to keep England in economic and political turmoil until the end of the 1840s began in 1837, almost at the same time he finished *The French Revolution*. Although *The French Revolution* depicted the failure of the French to author a constitution and become epic, it created an English audience that was willing to listen to Carlyle. Carlyle now sought to shape this audience, which was as yet the unheroic product of the era of revolution, into an epic nation. He wrote *Chartism* and *Past and Present* toward the beginning of this epoch, when he had the greatest confidence in his ability to use his writing to effect this change. "The Negro Question" and *Latter-Day Pamphlets*, written at the end of the period when he had lost his confidence, brought his reputation to the nadir of his writing career. Throughout this period, he was absorbed in the history of the Puritan era. From December 1838, when he began reading up on the Protectorate, until the denouement of the

Squire papers controversy in December 1849, Cromwell dominated Carlyle's thoughts and writings as he sought, unsuccessfully, to create his English epic.

From Literature to Polity

Carlyle had once hoped that literature would constitute belief that would in turn constitute social order, but, having found that the search for belief endlessly defers closure, he began to shift his focus from literature to politics, from discovering the author of a myth to discovering political authority. In shifting from novel to history, from the question of individual faith to the problem of social belief, he had steadily become more interested in problems of polity rather than of literature. In the 1820s, when he was neglecting history in favor of literature, he was indifferent to politics, and in the early 1830s he continued to hold himself apart from the political issues of the day, professing indifference to the elections that followed the Reform Bill in 1832, 1834, and 1835 (*CL*, 6:284, 7:197, 8:20). He did favor reform—after the first reform bill in 1831 was defeated he wondered whether it was his "duty" to speak out rather than "stand aloof"—but he had little faith in the kind of reform sought by the Whig establishment (*TNB*, 203; see *CL*, 6:52). Indeed, he regarded the onset of the recession in 1837 as a sign that the Reform Bill had failed. In *The French Revolution*, which he completed that year, he had adopted a more political orientation toward the problem of authority than he had in *Sartor Resartus*. For the first time, he became interested in the outcome of the elections, and by the early 1840s he was willing to acknowledge that his "nature was Political" (*CL*, 9:277; *NL*, 1:282).[2]

In the spring of 1838, when the Chartist movement began, Carlyle conceived the idea of writing a "Discourse on the Working Classes" (*CL*, 10:15). Convinced that it was his duty to "address . . . English fellow-men on the condition of men in England," he continued for the next year to contemplate how to formulate his thoughts (*CL*, 10:224, n. 14; see 11:104, 218, 235). While the Chartists were meeting in London to petition Parliament in the spring of 1839, he was lecturing in Portman Square on revolutions in modern Europe. Carlyle considered Chartism the latest rebirth of the revolution; the material of Chartism, he wrote, exists "in the hearts of all our working population, and would right gladly body itself in *any* promising shape; but Chartism begins to seem *un*promising. What to do with it? Yes, there is the question. Europe has been struggling to give some answer, very audibly since the year 1789" (*CL*, 11:160–61). He was not interested in the Chartists' proposals for electoral reform, but he felt that Chartism manifested genuine social problems which could not be ignored. When, in August, Parliament rejected the Chartist petition, he felt compelled to demonstrate the importance of the movement. He immediately set to work, completing his long essay in three months.

Carlyle wanted to address this discourse to those who were most likely to provide a solution to England's problems, but he was uncertain who that would be. If English society was fragmented, as he claimed it was, he had to determine which segment of society to address. As did his fellow citizens, he tended to see the divisions in English society in terms of the existing parliamentary parties. In deciding who might best lead England and whom he should therefore address, he felt he must decide among the speculative radicals, the Whigs, and the Tories.

Although he had written for periodicals associated with all three parties, Carlyle was most intimately connected with the Whigs. He was a friend of Francis Jeffrey who, as editor of the *Edinburgh Review*, published his first major reviews, but he had always been considered something of a maverick by its Whig readership, and soon after Jeffrey passed the editorship on to Macvey Napier in 1829, Carlyle's relationship with the *Edinburgh* ended. At the same time, Carlyle was becoming increasingly suspicious of the utilitarian bent of Whig reform, and he had no sympathy for the Enlightenment ideals of Lord Melbourne, who became prime minister in 1834. His disenchantment became complete in the later 1830s, when the complacent Whig majority began to oppose further reform. Since his essay would make them his principal target and he had little hope of changing their policies, he made no attempt to address them or to seek a Whig vehicle for his thoughts. More likely vehicles for his essay on Chartism were the respectable Tory *Quarterly Review*—he was now avoiding the "fat *glar* [mud] of Fraser's Toryism"—and the "unfruitful rubbish-mound of Mill's Radicalism" (*CL*, 9:76).

For a time, Carlyle had some hope that the Whigs' allies, the speculative radicals, might be converted into a more satisfactory reform party (*CL*, 5:280; see 11:222). Yet his feelings toward the radicals were even more sharply divided than his feelings about the Whigs. In the early 1830s, he frequently identified himself, like Teufelsdröckh, as a radical, and as late as 1837 he insisted that he was still radical, only averse to Benthamite "Formulism" (*CL*, 6:154, 183, 9:338). It was just that there was no "*right* Radicalism" (*CL*, 9:256). Comparing the radicals to the *philosophe*-inspired Girondins, he found in both "Formalism, hidebound Pedantry, superficiality, narrowness, barrenness" as well as the same "cold clean-washed patronising talk about 'the masses'" (*CL*, 9:69; see 187, 294; *FR*, 1:33). Unable to accept their insistence on rational utility as the basis for law and government, he hoped at first to convert them from speculative to "mystical" radicalism. For a time he even thought that he might found a "mystico-radical school" by becoming editor of the new radical journal (*CL*, 5:338, 6:72, 7:80–81, 218). But Mill and his friends were too committed to Benthamite principles to award the editorship to a man who detested the principle of utility, and Carlyle was not even given the opportunity to contribute to the *London and Westminster Review* until 1837 (Kaplan, 215). Nonetheless, because he shared with the radicals a desire for reform and because he still hoped to influence them, Carlyle approached Mill with his project of writing on Chartism when he first conceived it in 1838. But when Mill refused to listen to his criticisms of the radicals' project, Carlyle concluded that he could not write for the *London and Westminster*.[3]

Instead, he wrote to John Gibson Lockhart, proposing an article for the *Quarterly Review*. It appeared that the Tories were about to regain power, and Carlyle wanted to provide them with a political program.[4] When he became dissatisfied with Whig policies, he began to reconsider his antipathy to the Tories, whom he had been happy to see turned out in 1832 (*CL*, 6:307). His desire for a hierarchical social order made the principle of the aristocracy appealing to him even though he had little respect for the existing peerage. Since his views on the working class differed "intensely from those of the speculating radicals, intensely from those of the Whigs," he now found that "the better class of the Conservatives were on the whole the persons to whom it were hopefullest and in many ways fittest to address [him]self," that by "addressing" them, he could "awaken [them] to quite a *new* sense of their duties" (*CL*, 11:104, 12:11; see 117). Yet, with the exception of the romantic Tory Richard Monckton Milnes, Carlyle had no friends in the Tory party, and they were not about to be told what to do by a writer who had a long association with the

Whigs and radicals. When Lockhart turned down his proposal, he had no choice but to issue *Chartism* as a pamphlet at his own expense (see also Richardson).

Chartism and the Rhetoric of Partisanship

Carlyle's attempt to find a place for *Chartism* in the political reviews reveals the extent to which he conceived his discussion of the condition of England in terms of the analyses and solutions offered by the dominant political parties. He still hoped to awaken the Tories to their duty, but by publishing on his own he was free to write an essay "equally astonishing to Girondin Radicals, Donothing Aristocrat Conservatives, and Unbelieving Dilettante Whigs" (*CL*, 11:218; see 226, 10:104, 111, 117). Although the style of *Chartism* is distinctively Carlylean, Carlyle confined himself to the discourse of Parliament and the political reviews, the discourse of political economy rather than the ethical discourse of quasi-religious belief. Of course, Carlyle wanted to reshape and extend the boundaries of political discourse as well as to reshape the parties. If he had wanted to make the radicals mystics, he wanted to make the Tories radical (since the parties themselves were unstable at this period, undergoing major transformation, this aim was not as unrealistic as it may first appear). He was happy to find that the first notices of *Chartism*, in the Whig *Morning Chronicle* and the Tory *Spectator*, recognized his new Toryism, what the radical *Tait's Edinburgh Review* called "radical Toryism" (*CL*, 12:3–4; Seigel, 165).[5]

From the beginning, Carlyle intended to attack the utilitarian principles embodied in reform legislation like the Poor Law of 1834, and *Chartism* continues an argument with Mill on this question that began in their correspondence concerning it. When Carlyle informed Mill that his essay would criticize the New Poor Law, Mill had defended the law by citing the improved condition of the working class.[6] Carlyle replied that under present circumstances "it is a bitter mockery to talk of 'improvement'" (*CL*, 10:15). Carlyle saw this as a key issue in the radical position, claiming, a year later, that Mill had refused to publish his essay unless he "would come to the conclusion that *their situation was gradually improving!*" (*CL*, 11:117; see 12:11). In *Chartism*, Carlyle adapted his reply to Mill to attack the "cruel mockery" of the principles underlying radical reform legislation (*CME*, 4:142).

Yet although it attacks the utilitarians, *Chartism* employs the utilitarian mode of argument. For example, Carlyle argued that the condition of the working class was growing worse, rather than improving, because a growing labor pool and the displacement of labor by machinery were steadily reducing the value of labor and ruining living conditions (*CME*, 4:141). Instead of questioning the validity of classical economics, this argument uses one of its basic principles—the effect of the supply of labor on wages—to attack the arguments of the radicals. Similarly, Carlyle criticized the New Poor Law not because it dehumanized poor relief (he approved of several of the radicals' innovations, including centralized administration and the principle of encouraging work), but because it erroneously assumed that work was available for all able-bodied individuals, once again an issue of supply and demand. Although he did occasionally set aside the plain style of rational argument and made affective appeals to the reader, he used these appeals only to heighten his argument, not to undermine utilitarian discourse (e.g., *CME*, 4:141–42).

The rhetorical strategy of *Chartism* is most limiting when it comes to articulating solutions. While it effectively attacks laissez-faire, it is much less successful in envisioning the new social order. Indeed, because the critique of utilitarianism, which was implicit rather than explicit, overwhelms the discussion of the need for authority, reviewers tended to miss it. Focusing instead on Carlyle's more specific proposals for a national system of education to improve the condition of the working class and a national program for emigration to reduce the size of the labor pool, they were quick to criticize his solutions as vague, impractical, even unoriginal.[7] On the last count, at least, they were justified; both programs had been debated in Parliament for years. Carlyle's support for these programs—which he regarded as ways in which the government could assert its authority—demonstrates the extent to which the arguments of *Chartism* were dictated by the parameters of parliamentary debate. (When Carlyle repeated these proposals in *Past and Present*, he was to stress that they were only examples of what an authoritative government might attempt to do, not solutions in themselves.) His attraction to the old aristocracy, the existing Tory party, raises the same questions. He was not unaware that, as Lady Sydney Morgan pointed out, the same Tory aristocracy that had just a few months earlier staged the absurd Eglinton tournament hardly seemed likely to be converted to radicalism (29). *Chart-ism* itself concludes with the complaint that instead of providing the leadership England needed, the aristocracy was busy preserving game (*CL*, 4:204).

Carlyle did not achieve a vision of the recovery of authority in *Chartism* because he confined himself to a discourse that he considered part of the problem. *Chartism*, like *The French Revolution*, criticizes the endless speech-making of parliaments, but rather than providing an alternative to parliamentary discourse it reinforces the terms of the parliamentary debate (see *CME*, 4:168; *CL*, 11:43). Furthermore, Carlyle only gets as far as "gird[ing]" himself "up for actual doing"; his discourse neither acts on the English people nor shows them how to act (*CME*, 4:190; see P. Rosenberg, 138). Like the discourse of the Girondins and radicals, the discourse of *Chartism* is effective in undermining the status quo but does not enable one to envision a new social order. No wonder that the *Monthly Chronicle* found Carlyle's "creed . . . without hope—his labour without progression" (107).

The "Hero as King" and the Idyll as Theocracy

Carlyle continued to seek a literary form through which he could envision and represent the recuperation of authority. Even as the first reviews of *Chartism* were appearing, he was looking forward to a new series of lectures that would give him the opportunity to formulate a theory of the cyclical rise and fall of social authority. While his previous lectures had for the most part reworked older material, he would for the first time use his lectures to work out an idea that would be worth "promulgat[ing] . . . farther" as a book (*CL*, 12:184).[8]

With *On Heroes and Hero-Worship*, Carlyle shifted the locus of authority from the realm of literature to the realm of politics, a shift manifested in a last-minute change in the order of the lectures. He initially planned to end the series with a lecture on Burns, but sometime between April 11, when he began writing notes for the lectures, and May 5, when the lectures began, he altered his plan and decided to conclude with a lecture on Cromwell and Napoleon (*CL*, 12:103, 115, 128).[9] In addition to demonstrating the importance he would give to the hero as king, this change indicates that, as Carlyle himself admitted, the lectures were "not so much historic as didactic" (*CL*, 12:94).

We must read them not as a history of authority, but as a history of Carlyle's own attempt to envision a new form of authority.

   Through the figure of the hero, Carlyle attempted to resolve the tension between transcendence and history. The hero is simultaneously transcendental, in that he always embodies the same transcendental authority, and historical, in that the embodiment belongs to a specific time, place, and culture. While all eleven figures discussed in the lectures are heroes—that is, possess transcendental authority— their authority takes six different historical forms: the hero as divinity, prophet, poet, priest, man of letters, and king. At times, the dual nature of the hero amounts to a contradiction rather than a resolution of the tension between historical and transcendental authority. When Carlyle argues that all the heroes are "originally of one stuff" and that Mirabeau could have been a poet and Burns a politician, he tends to deprive them of their historical specificity (43, 79). By contrast, the historicity of the individual heroic types puts into question his assertion that, since the hero transcends history, any hero could appear in any era. Carlyle attempts to resolve the tension between transcendence and history through the form of *On Heroes*. The four heroes following the hero as divinity become enmeshed in their historical era, and, by the time the hero as man of letters appears, transcendental authority has nearly disappeared. The final lecture, on the hero as king, attempts to escape history and recuperate authority by circling back to the first, the hero as divinity.[10]

   The hero as divinity has a privileged position in the sequence of heroes. Whereas the other heroes manifest divinity in human form, Odin represents unmediated transcendental authority itself. The embodiment of both religious and political authority, he can create an aboriginal language through which belief becomes social order. He is, in effect, the God of Genesis creating the Garden of Eden.

   Only Odin can be the originary creator; the succeeding heroes belong to the postlapsarian era. The Odin-like qualities that these later heroes possess increasingly become submerged in their historical roles. They must first destroy the remains of the historical mediations through which authority had been transmitted in the preceding era and then recreate society out of the remains of these mediations. But, like the French during the revolution, they have difficulty in shifting from destruction to creation. Mahomet the iconoclast, rather than

Odin, is the model for the succeeding heroes (120, 132–33, 199–200). (In "The Hero as Poet," Mahomet appears nine times, Odin only once; in "The Hero as Priest," Luther is compared to Odin once but to Mahomet several times.) If Mahomet can still create a theocracy, Knox fails to do so, the hero as priest "revers[ing]" the work of previous heroes who have "buil[t] . . . Religions" (151–52, 116). While Carlyle wants to argue that each hero fully recovers the authority of his predecessor, that time and history do not make a difference, he cannot avoid noticing that his lectures represent the steady diminishment of authority: "The Hero taken as Divinity; the Hero taken as Prophet; then next the Hero taken only as Poet: does it not look as if our estimate of the Great Man, epoch after epoch, were continually diminishing? We take him first for a god, then for one god-inspired; and now in the next stage of it, his most miraculous word gains from us only the recognition that he is a Poet, beautiful verse-maker, man of genius, or such like!" (84). The latter heroes inaugurate the revolutionary era of destruction.[11]

By the time we reach the man of letters, the hero is completely enmeshed in history and revolution, his transcendental authority diminished almost to nothing. While the hero as divinity is no longer possible, the man of letters had never been possible before; he belongs to history, not to all times (154). In "The Hero as Man of Letters," we can see Carlyle revising the representation of the literary man that he had borrowed from Fichte twenty years earlier. Although he begins by repeating Fichte's idea that the man of letters manifests a "divine idea," the remainder of the lecture demonstrates that he no longer believes in the authority of the writer.[12] Whereas the hero as poet, the Dante or Shakespeare, could create an epic for an era of belief, Johnson, Rousseau, and Burns belong to a century dominated by unbelief. Johnson and Rousseau both produce gospels, but Johnson's "Gospel . . . of Moral Prudence" is so firmly embedded in history that it is already dead by Carlyle's time, and Rousseau's "evangel" has produced unbelief, the opposite of social order (182). Carlyle's original intention to conclude with a lecture on Burns, a figure with whom he closely identified, indicates that he may have been planning a more optimistic representation of the man of letters. But instead of portraying the man of letters as the savior of the modern era, the lecture portrays him as a symptom of its problems. Burns, like Rousseau and Johnson, seeks authority and does not find it; he attempts to shape the world but is shaped by it (158). The man of letters is not a hero in the same sense that his predecessors were; he is a mere "Half-Hero" (171).

If Carlyle had wished to portray the modern man of letters as possessor of transcendental authority, as at least the equivalent of the hero as poet, he could have chosen Goethe as his exemplar. In fact, the choice was so obvious that he felt compelled to explain the exclusion of Goethe at the outset of the lecture. Yet his stated reason, that Goethe was too little known to be understood in England, is odd, to say the least, coming from the man who had done so much to make Goethe known there.[13] The exclusion of Goethe suggests that Carlyle had lost faith in Goethe's authority, particularly in his ability to create a new social order through his art. Johnson, Rousseau, and Burns, he seems to say, represent all that the man of letters can really achieve.

That Carlyle should discover in the hero as king the figure who recovers the transcendental authority of the hero as divinity is just as surprising as his exclusion of Goethe in "The Hero as Man of Letters."[14] In *The French Revolution*, he had demonstrated that monarchy, at least feudal monarchy, was dead, but, although both Cromwell and Napoleon ruled nations, neither was, strictly speaking, a "king." Carlyle chose them to represent, not feudal monarchy, but the reinvention of kingship in the era of revolution. In effect, the hero as lawmaker supplants the hero as culture-maker, the wielder of the sword, the wielder of words.

The hero as king is "a kind of God" who recovers the transcendental authority of the hero as divinity and the lost transcendental idyll. But in order to recover this "ideal country," this "perfect state" of theocracy, the king must escape the mediations of history that have encumbered his predecessors (198, 197). Instead of manifesting the transcendental in writing, he must put it directly into action. The sequence of heroes from Odin to the men of letters are all authors whose writing projects manifest their diminishing authority. Odin is literally the first man of letters, creating an alphabet with which to record mythology (27–28). Mahomet writes the Koran, which Carlyle had equated in "On Biography" with foundational cultural myths like the Bible and the *Iliad*. Dante and Shakespeare record the spiritual and secular epics of their culture, Christianity and chivalry, in *The Divine Comedy* and the *Henriad*. But Luther can do no more than translate the Bible, a mythus that is already losing its authority; and, while Johnson, Rousseau, and Burns produce "letters"—one thinks especially of Johnson's dictionary—they are incapable of creating myth or epic. Cromwell and Napoleon break the pattern. With them the hero becomes an actor, not a writer. Neither Cromwell, who puts an end to the parliamentary speech-making that endlessly defers creation of his theocracy, nor Napoleon, who puts an end to the Terror, mediates the transcendental ideal through a finite text; both translate it directly into the social order through action (229–34).

The movement from man of letters or religious leader to king or political leader manifests not only a shift from writing to action, but a shift from the priority of belief that informs social order to the priority of law that enforces social order. The first three lectures portray eras in which belief creates a social order, the eras of paganism, Islam, and Christianity. The last three lectures portray eras in which revolution prevents the creation of social order. Luther and Knox attempt to establish a new theocracy but fail because they have destroyed the authority of the pope (199–200). The medieval theocracy in which the religious authority of the pope took precedence over the secular authority of kings—represented by the submission of Emperor Henry IV to Pope Hildebrand at Canossa, Henry acknowledging that "the world [i.e., Henry as king] could have no legitimate control in things spiritual"—was no longer viable in an era of revolution (*HL*, 74; see *HHW*, 152). In the "Hero as King," royal authority subsumes religious authority; the king with "something of the Pontiff in him," rather than the pope, will put the spiritual into practice as "head of the *Church*" (199). Britain needs more than Knox the priest, Carlyle decides; it needs Cromwell the king (*CL*, 12:150).[15]

Yet while the people obey the hero as divinity because they believe in what he says, they obey the hero as king because he compels them by "weight and force" (231). Carlyle would have it that the king's actions manifest his transcendental authority—that the hero as king is not fundamentally different from the hero as divinity, since all heroes reveal the divine law—yet it turns out that we do not know how to recognize this authority (230, 234). "It is a fearful business," he concludes, "that of having your Able-man to *seek*, and not knowing in what manner to proceed about it!" (199). Carlyle calls for hero-worship, but he cannot show us how to find or recognize a hero.

On Heroes and Hero-Worship elides these difficulties in its culminating vision of the recovery of authority by the hero as king who recovers the domain of unmediated belief and returns us to the prelapsarian idyll of the hero as divinity. In this regard, at least, *On Heroes* succeeds where *Chartism* had failed, enabling Carlyle to imagine a new class of leaders, modern heroes, who would play a central role in his new epic for modern England. At the same time, however, the figure of the hero as king, which would dominate his writings for the rest of his life, marks the limits and underlies the failure of his social vision.

Cromwell Past and Present

Another way to explain the anachronism of concluding *On Heroes and Hero-Worship* with Cromwell is to say that Carlyle did not consider Cromwell part of the past but a hero for the present. Since the end of 1838 he had been considering whether the Puritan era might be the subject of his next book, presenting his first public defense of Cromwell in his lectures on modern revolutions in the spring of 1839, and then concluding the lectures on heroes with Cromwell the following year (*CL*, 11:246).[16] Immediately after completing those lectures, he began reading extensively about the civil wars and Cromwell, whom he now regarded as the "last (King) *Könning* of England" (*CL*, 14:8, n. 4). He wanted to do more than write a history, however; he wanted quite literally to bring Cromwell back to life, to "save a hero for [his] country."[17] Convinced that "the one hope of help" for his "own poor generation . . . consisted in the possibility of new Cromwells and new Puritans," he "pray[ed] daily for a new Oliver" (*RWE*, 328; *CL*, 14:184; see 210). The Puritan revolution was incomplete because the settlement of 1660 had turned back the clock and restored the old social order. Carlyle sought to complete the revolution in his own era by restoring Cromwell's reputation and encouraging the emergence of a Cromwellian hero.

To achieve this goal, Carlyle needed to create a "new [literary] form from centre to surface" that would make epic history reshape the present as well as reflect the past (*LL*, 1:300). Since he regarded history as epic—what the present believes to be true—history was as much concerned with the present as with the past. The problem was that, just as the Puritan revolution had been suspended by the settlement of 1660, so the making of the English epic had been suspended by the failure of English authors. England had the material for an epic history, Carlyle lamented, but English literature had failed to speak "what the gods were pleased to act"; instead of an epic or Bible, it had produced only a "Collins's Peerage and the illegible torpedo rubbish mounds" of dry-as-dust histories (Fielding and Tarr, 18). Just as he hoped to inspire the emergence of a new Cromwell, so he hoped that his history of the Puritan revolution would provide an epic for the nineteenth century. The "seventeenth" century is "*worthless*," he concluded, "except precisely in so far as it can be made the *nineteenth*" (*RWE*, 328).[18]

Yet Carlyle did not succeed in creating the "new form" he needed. "No work I ever tried gets on worse with me than this of Cromwell," he wrote. "I know not for my life in what way to take it up, how to get into the heart of it, what on earth to do with it. For many months I have lain at it beleaguering it; literally girdling in all sides; watching if on any side there might be found admittance into it" (fol. 95 and v.). He complained repeatedly that it was "impossible" to discover the reality of Puritan history beneath the documentary "rubbish mounds" it had left behind (*CL*, 14:229; see *LL*, 1:299, 360; *RWE*, 350).[19] Although he wanted to believe that Cromwell could still live for the present, he discovered that his hero was locked away in the inaccessible past and often complained that the Puritan revolution could not be made as interesting as the French Revolution because it was not, like the latter, still alive in the minds of his contemporaries (*CL*, 11:15, 12:305, 14:8; Fielding and Tarr, 16).[20]

Between 1839, when he began working on Cromwell, and 1844, when he decided merely to edit Cromwell's letters and speeches, Carlyle continued unsuccessfully to seek a literary form that would merge past and present.[21] He tried to create scenes like the "Procession" in *The French Revolution*, to find a structural nucleus for the history in a list of "Moments" and a dramatic scenario, even to write "rhyme," but none of these attempts made Cromwell come alive (Forster, fols. 93, 105 v., 154; *LL*, 1:299).[22] The difficulties manifest themselves in a brief passage that literally attempts to revive Cromwell as a ghost speaking, like the ghost of Hamlet's father, to the modern-day sons of England: "Not Christ's Gospel now, and a Godly Ministry; but the People's Charter and Free Trade in Corn. My Poor beloved countrymen,—alas, Priests have become chimerical, and your Lords . . . do stick the stubble ground with dry bushes in preservation of their partridges" (Fielding and Tarr, 16). Instead of uniting the centuries, however, Cromwell's seventeenth-century syntax jars against the incongruous nineteenth-century vocabulary, sounding ridiculous rather than portentous. Part of Carlyle's problem was that, whereas *The French Revolution* had been dominated by speech, he intended the book on Cromwell to be dominated by action. At one point, he attempted to emphasize action by casting the history in the form of an epic drama in twelve acts.[23] Yet, although King Charles's flight, like the "Night of Spurs" in *The French Revolution*, provided "a dramatic scene," on the whole he found that the history of the civil wars contained "no *action*" and was "not *dramatic*" (9–10). Cromwell's battles would provide action, but not of a very dramatic or symbolic kind, and, in the end, nearly half of the scenario dramatizes squabbles between Cromwell and Parliament, exactly what Carlyle wanted to avoid.

Already in 1841, as he saw England slipping into the worst economic recession of the century, Carlyle was becoming discouraged with his failure to make any progress on Cromwell. In May of 1842, as he journeyed to and from Scotland, he was struck by the sight of idle factories in Manchester and disturbed by his encounters with impoverished farm laborers (*CL*, 14:178, 183–84). When the Tories finally regained power in 1841, he had predicted that Peel would quickly abrogate the Corn Laws, but Peel was slow to act (*CL*, 13:139).[24] In the spring of 1842, Parliament once again refused to receive a Chartist petition, and that summer riots and disturbances spread throughout the country, even into his native Annandale (*CL*, 14:214). Carlyle concluded that England needed a "very different sort" of prime minister, "a new Oliver" (*CL*, 14:184; see 24, 39, 224).

In August, on the anniversary of Peterloo, Carlyle noted, there was a workers' insurrection in Manchester (Bliss, 152). Five days later, noting that the insurrection was still going on, he informed Jane Carlyle that he was "writing, writing; God knows at what precisely" (Bliss, 153). He had begun *Past and Present*.[25] Determined to use the past to address the nation on the subject of this crisis, he abandoned Cromwell and the seventeenth century in favor of Abbot Samson and the twelfth. While visiting sites associated with Cromwell that autumn, he saw in the contrast between the St. Ives workhouse and the nearby ruins of the abbey of St. Edmund the relationship between past and present he had been seeking to illustrate.[26] After trying to write about Cromwell for more than three years without success, he completed *Past and Present*, his most powerful piece of social criticism, in just a few months.

While the use of the past in *Past and Present* was to provide him with the vision of an alternative society that had been lacking in *Chartism*, Carlyle also needed to determine how to address his audience. By addressing existing political parties in *Chartism*, he had confined himself to the factional politics of the present. In *Past and Present* he turned to England's ruling classes, the aristocratic landowners and middle-class industrialists themselves, rather than to the parties that represented them in Parliament. While *Chartism* sought to create radical Tories, *Past and Present* would attempt to transform wealthy industrialists into captains of industry.

This strategy evolved in dialogue with the critics of *Chartism*, particularly William Sewell in the *Quarterly Review* and Herman Merivale in the *Edinburgh Review*. Although Sewell and Carlyle had little in common, each found something to like about the other.[27] Carlyle had little respect for Sewell's Pusey-inspired faith in the Church of England, but he preferred Sewell's belief in a dead religion to Merivale's radical "atheism" (*CL*, 12:282; see 292). For Carlyle, Merivale's insistence that government intervention could not eliminate hunger was tantamount to arguing that since "starvation and misery among the poorer classes is perpetual and eternal . . . all good Government consists in uniting of the monied classes to keep down that one miserable class, and make the pigs *die without squealing*" (*CL*, 12:204; see 206, 264, 282, 291–92).[28] Carlyle would borrow Sewell's theological discourse to counter the bloodless reasoning of Merivale's utilitarianism and to provide an ethical center for his analysis of contemporary society.

At the same time, Carlyle did not intend to address the Tories again; instead, he envisioned a governing class that would combine the hierarchical leadership and religious faith of the Tories with the Whig Radicals' industry and drive for reform. Rather than appealing to politicians, he would appeal to industrialists, demanding that they make principles of justice the foundation of their business practices: "we must have industrial *barons*, of a quite new suitable sort; workers *loyally* related to their taskmasters,—related in God . . . not related in Mammon alone! This will be the real aristocracy" (*CL*, 13:317). Carlyle wrote this to James Garth Marshall of the Marshall family that had already been influenced by his writings and had attempted to implement some of his principles at Temple Mill. In Carlyle's letters to Marshall, which are clearly intended to inspire Marshall to become a captain of industry, we can see Carlyle beginning to envision the principal audience of *Past and Present*. In men like Marshall and the Quaker manufacturer mentioned in Chadwick's report for the Poor Law Commission, Carlyle thought he saw the "beginning of a real Industrial *Baron*hood" (*CL*, 13:325).[29]

In 1842 when he began *Past and Present*, Carlyle had every reason to believe that his analyses and solutions would be taken seriously; his reputation had never been greater, and his authority was already being used to support calls for reform. The previous October, he learned that the editor of the *Manchester Times* had reprinted his description of the riots that had touched off the French Revolution as a "Plea for the Poor" (*CL*, 13:278). Later that autumn, in the conclusion of his essay on *The Letters and Journals of Robert Baillie*, he made his first public attempt to make the past speak to the present when he ironically compared the "divine right" of country squires—the staunchest defenders of the Corn Laws—to profit at the expense of the poor to the divine right of kings (*CME*, 4:259). The satirical passage was taken up by the newspapers and widely reprinted under the title "The Divine Right of Squires." Carlyle was clearly pleased that a "word of [his]" might "help to relieve the world from an unsupportable oppression" (*CL*, 14:7). He was also pleased when his sister asked if he were going to be made "king." Although he replied that there was no "danger" of that eventuality, he had, in fact, long enjoyed imagining what he would do if "they were to make [him] Cromwell of it all" (*CL*, 14:47).[30] He knew he could not be made king, but he could at least use his words to inspire another to become the new Cromwell.

Past and Present: Epic as Action

The form of *Past and Present* has two functions, to bring the past into the present—to recover the lost idyll—and to convert its audience— to represent the audience's movement from the present into a future that recuperates the past. *Past and Present* does not simply analyze the condition of England, it *represents* that condition by depicting the various factions that make up English society in much the same way that *The French Revolution* had dramatized the voices of conflicting factions. Through dialogue between the prophetic author and the factions dividing English society, Carlyle imagines the conversion of his contemporaries and the emergence of a new era. In order to represent the audience's movement from the present into the future, he divides *Past and Present* into visions of how an idyllic monastery was recovered by an "Ancient Monk" in the past, an analysis of the conditions facing "The Modern Worker" in the present, and a "Horoscope" of the future. In the process, *Past and Present* transforms epic as myth

or text into epic as fertile nation, enabling Carlyle to imagine the recuperation of the lost idyll but also introducing the authoritarianism
that was to become predominant in *Latter-Day Pamphlets* and *Frederick
the Great*.

A new voice reflecting Carlyle's heightened sense of authority domi-
nates the dialogues of *Past and Present*. Neither the Editor of *Sartor
Resartus* nor Teufelsdröckh presumes to claim that what he says is
"A God's-message," that "It is Fact, speaking once more, in miraculous thunder-voice, from out of the centre of the world." Like the
prophet, this speaker claims to bear a "God's message" and threatens divine retribution: "Behold, ye shall grow wiser, or ye shall die!"
(34). For the first time, the persona of the Carlylean narrator fully
assumes the role of prophet who can speak with the transcendental
authority of "Fact," "Nature," "the Universe," "Nature's eternal law,"
"the Heavens," or "the Highest God" (34; 160–61, 184, 187; 182, 217;
221; 269; 279, 281).

The prophetic narrator of *Past and Present* addresses his audience
as if he were delivering a sermon. The narrator of *Chartism* had been
a variation on the editorial voice of the political reviews for which
Carlyle originally intended it. Its dominant tone is that of the dis-
embodied voice of reason rather than Carlyle at his most characteristic: "A witty statesman said, you might prove anything by figures.
We have looked into various statistic works, Statistic-Society Reports,
Poor-Law Reports, Reports and Pamphlets not a few, with a sedulous
eye to this question of the Working Classes and their general condition in England; we grieve to say, with as good as no result whatever"
(*CME*, 4:124). Typically, this speaker does not address his audience as
if he were speaking to it directly, but the narrator of *Past and Present*,
seeking an immediate relationship with the members of his audience,
addresses them as "brothers": "O brother, can it be needful now, at
this late epoch of experience, after eighteen centuries of Christian
preaching for one thing, to remind thee of such a fact; which all manner of Mahometans, old Pagan Romans, Jews, Scythians and heathen
Greeks . . . have managed at one time to see into; nay which thou
thyself, till 'red-tape' strangled the inner life of thee, hadst once some
inkling of: That there *is* justice here below; and even, at bottom, that
there is nothing else but justice!" (*PP*, 14). The archaic diction of the
passage—with its echoes of the King James Bible—is not the language
of the respectable political review but of the pulpit. *Past and Present*

does not address its appeal to members of Parliament but seeks a broader constituency of middle- and upper-class readers, for many of whom the ethical discourse of the Bible remained as powerful as the discourse of political economy.

But although Carlyle thunders like a prophet, he does not wish to isolate himself from his congregation as Irving had done, and so he imagines dialogues between himself and his audience. As in *The French Revolution*, where he represented the conflicting voices of revolutionary factions, he creates a range of personae, personifications, and types who represent all sides of the debate about the condition of England. But, whereas in *The French Revolution* he could only apostrophize historical actors whose actions were already fixed in the past, in *Past and Present* he could hope to shape the future actions of his audience. This enabled him to organize *Past and Present* as a dialectical narrative through which he shapes his audience into a new class responsible for the salvation of England. In addition to adopting the role of the prophet, he represents himself as an observer with a unique, but not necessarily transcendental, perspective, as Diogenes Teufelsdröckh, Gottfried Sauerteig, a picturesque tourist who visits the St. Ives workhouse, and a newspaper reporter for the *Houndsditch Indicator*. Ranged against him are the sausage-maker Bobus Higgins of Houndsditch, the landlord of Castle-Rackrent, the industrial Firm of Plugson, Hunks and Company in St. Dolly Undershot, Pandarus Dogdraught, Aristides Rigmarole Esq. of the Destructive Party, the Hon. Alcides Dolittle of the Conservative Party, black Quashee, Haiti Duke of Marmalade, the merchant Sam Slick, Mecænas Twiddledee, and the continental newspaper editors Blusterowski, Colacorde and company.[31] Carlyle's use of dramatized discussion suggests that his audience is not being coerced by a superior power, but persuaded by the truths he reveals to them. These dialogues constitute a metanarrative in which Carlyle's readers, initially opposed to him, eventually come to understand and believe him, narrator and audience merging in the concluding vision of social union.

In book 1 of *Past and Present*, entitled "Proem," Carlyle reads the symbols and signs of the times in order to create a mythic framework for his analysis of the condition of England. As in *The French Revolution*, the titles of the chapters—"Midas," "The Sphinx," "Manchester Insurrection," "Morrison's Pill," and so on—emphasize symbolic interpretation rather than systematic inquiry. The opening paragraph,

for example, makes the same argument as the opening paragraph of
Chartism; but whereas *Chartism* simply states a thesis and elaborates
it analytically, *Past and Present* elaborates it mythically by comparing
England to Midas, "full of wealth . . . yet . . . dying of inanition" (7).
Furthermore, by focusing on the sudden loss "of unabated bounty,"
Carlyle not only begins to create a vision of the problems that beset
England, he also foretells the resolution in which bounty is restored.
From the beginning, *Past and Present* promises to use the vision of past
"bounty" in order to imagine a bountiful future.[32]

In the first half of book 1, Carlyle represents his audience as "idle
reader[s] of Newspapers" who might misread the signs of the times,
but he is more concerned to demonstrate a correct reading than to
attack his audience for its obtuseness (9). In order to enlighten his
audience about the condition of England, he attempts to give voice
to the mute working class, what the actions of the striking workers
in Manchester and the Stockport mother and father who killed their
children so they could collect burial insurance "think and hint" (10).[33]
The debate begins when Carlyle's audience asks, in response to his
claim that the working class is demanding action from them: "What is
to be done, what would you have us do?" (28). The concluding chapters of book 1 elaborate his reply to this question through dialogues
between his avatars and representatives of his audience. By creating,
in the ignorant "Bobus Higgins, Sausage-maker on the great scale,"
a comic caricature of the more fatuous elements of the middle class,
he is able to attack its narrow views of social reform while avoiding
a personal attack on his readers (35). Furthermore, by articulating
this attack through his fictional avatars, Gottfried Sauerteig and a
reporter for the *Houndsditch Indicator*, Carlyle avoids the appearance
that he is judging Bobus himself. This strategy enables him to concur
in his own voice with Bobus's demand for an "aristocracy of talent"
while broadening the demand to encompass revolutionary reform, a
"radical universal alteration of your regimen and way of life" (28;
see 41; Landow, *Elegant Jeremiahs*, 53–62). Creation of an aristocracy
of talent will not mean the establishment of a meritocracy that will
better serve Bobus's middle class, he suggests, but a transformation
of Bobuses into a "whole world of Heroes." To the reader's question,
"What is to be done," his ultimate response is that we must become
"hero-worshippers"; we must discover a hero who will lead us into the
promised land.

Book 2, "The Ancient Monk," represents one such revolutionary transformation as it was wrought by the heroic Abbot Samson. Samson's twelfth-century monastery, like English society of the nineteenth century, had lost sight of its original ideals and fallen into decay. The narrative of "The Ancient Monk" represents the recuperation of the lost idyll established by the ideals of St. Edmund three centuries before the arrival of Samson, the familiar circular narrative of the journey from idyll to exile and back again. This narrative sequence is, in turn, the model for the sequence of books 2–4. From the history of Abbot Samson, Carlyle shapes a vision of heroes who can reform their own society, or at least perhaps their factories, as Samson had reformed his twelfth-century monastery.

Carlyle's intention of bringing Cromwell back to life in the nineteenth century reveals itself in his representation of Samson as hero. He regarded Cromwell and Samson as similar men, his first writings on Samson appearing in the pages of his Cromwell manuscripts and Cromwell appearing throughout *Past and Present*.[34] The revolutions of Samson and Cromwell, unlike the French Revolution, transform society from above rather than from below, transmitting change downward through the hierarchy. Samson is not himself a king, but, like a king, he is not popularly elected. Furthermore, his appointment is authorized by the king, who plays a major role in selecting him to reside at the apex of the monastery's hierarchy. The reestablishment of the monastic hierarchy enables Samson to refurbish and revitalize the monastery.

Book 3, "The Modern Worker," represents the anarchic present through contentious dialogues between the narrator and his contemporaries. The dialogue form does not play an important role in book 2, presumably because the monks, even though they do not like all that Samson does, share a common system of belief and therefore have no need to argue with one another. The sequence of idyll/exile/idyll becomes the sequence of silence (no need for dialogue)/speech and dialogue/silence. The example of book 2 suggests that the dialogues of book 3 aim ultimately to move from conflict to unity, from speech to silence in book 4.

Because Carlyle uses the dialogues of book 3 to develop his critique of liberal democracy, he does not attempt to be even-handed in his representation of the opposition. Spokesmen for the aristocracy and middle class, for example, expose the weaknesses of their positions in the process of defending them and are readily refuted by the transcendental voices of "Nature" and the "Law" (e.g., 172–73, 193, 214). At the same time, because Carlyle's audience does not have the vision to understand England's plight, it remains polarized against him, unwilling to accept the solutions he offers. Throughout book 3, this tension between the narrator and the audience remains unchanged and appears to be irremediable. In *Chartism* this situation undermined Carlyle's attempts to envision the future; the ignorance of his audience could only lead to more ignorance, to more anarchy. The form of *Past and Present*, however, enables him to confine present-day anarchy to book 3 so that it does not contaminate his representation of the past or the future.

Carlyle's analysis of the condition of England also differs from that in *Chartism*, centering here on the ethical void created by the destruction of religious faith. At the center of the medieval world of Abbot Samson is the religious belief that forms the basis of the social order. At the center of his own world, Carlyle finds negation of belief, and from the negation of belief follows the negation of social order. He portrays the anarchy of democratic political institutions and the irresponsibility of laissez-faire economics, along with atheism, as absences or negations that make social order impossible. Rather than criticizing middle-class democracy on its own terms, Carlyle insists that democracy is the product of the "atheism" that has dominated English government since the restoration of 1660 (140–43, 149, 169). Similarly, he argues that the cash nexus of laissez-faire economics is "kin to *Atheism*," finding "Heart-Atheism," for example, in the empty symbol of the "huge lath-and-plaster hat" paraded through the streets of London to advertise a hat manufacturer (215, 148–50, 144). The utilitarians, and even his more orthodox contemporaries, Carlyle insists, are wrong to think that the problems of the socioeconomic order can be solved in isolation from the transcendental order.

The atheism discussed in *Past and Present*, then, is not so much a theological question as a question of moral order. Carlyle deplores the argument that economy determines the fundamental social order because it suggests that economy is morally neutral, driven by self-interest without respect to social values or a sense of social responsibility. He responds that government operating on the "No-God hypothesis" cannot infuse justice and truth into the social order. The "moral-sense" that makes individuals just and honest will not arise from within the socioeconomic order, but must be infused from above in the form of religious belief. "Money" has destroyed the "moral-sense," he concludes, turning "masses of mankind" into "egoists" who "cut [themselves] with triumphant completeness forever loose from [their employees], by paying down certain shillings and pounds" (194, 189).

Whereas government, the realm of the political, ought to be the means whereby the transcendental moral order is infused into the chaos of human society, democracy merely institutionalizes the social anarchy of laissez-faire economics (see 89–90, 153, 214–18). When the market is left "free" to regulate itself, the wealthy exploit their economic "might" with no more sense of moral obligation than "Buca-niers and Chactaws"; it is democracy, not monarchy, that validates the "Law of the Stronger" (26; see 191ff.). Laissez-faire offers only the very limited "freedom" to seek the best work, a freedom that becomes in times of dearth merely the "Liberty to die by starvation" (211). Furthermore, because this freedom forces laborers to compete with one another for work, it produces profound "social isolation": it "is to live miserable we know not why; to work sore and yet gain nothing; to be heart-worn, weary, yet isolated, unrelated . . . to die slowly all our life long, imprisoned in a deaf, dead, Infinite Injustice" (218, 210).[35]

The intransigence of the parties with whom Carlyle debates the condition of England question in book 3 represents the fundamental self-interestedness of individuals who lack the "moral-sense" as well as the divisive social fragmentation that follows from this social condi-tion; in book 4, "Horoscope," Carlyle's audience experiences the con-version he had called for in book 1, constituting itself as the captains of industry. They now acknowledge the narrator's transcendental au-thority and become once again believers in the transcendental order. The resulting unity of narrator and audience represents the recovery of social cohesion that is the precondition for recovering the tran-scendental idyll. Taking up its place in the new social hierarchy, the audience, too, becomes an authority and begins to govern justly and to create an idyllic England.

Past and Present calls on all elements of society to seek reform but specifically envisions the leaders of the reform movement as the indus-trial middle class transformed into captains of industry. In book 4, Carlyle represents the industrialists who had earlier sought to jus-tify their exploitation of the poor as discovering their moral self-degradation and the need for a domain of value: "I am encircled with squalor, with hunger, rage, and sooty desperation. . . . What good is it? My five hundred scalps hang here in my wigwam: would to Heaven

I had sought something else than the scalps; would to Heaven I had been a Christian Fighter, not a Chactaw one! . . . I will try for something other, or account my life a tragical futility!" (290–91). Thus the "moral-sense" is transmitted through the prophetic narrator of *Past and Present* to the new captains of industry, transcendental authority moving downward and outward, converting anarchy into a new social order. The dialogues of book 4 consequently pit reformed captains of industry against unreformed Bobuses rather than Carlyle against his contemporaries (291). Instead of defending the status quo, the speakers for this new class seek to reform England, prodding the government to act, rejecting the claims of vested interests, and denouncing the belief that "there is nothing but vulturous hunger, for fine wines, valet reputation and gilt carriages" (268; see 257, 262, 267). Just as Teufelsdröckh discovers that his vocation is to "Be no longer a Chaos, but a World," to create "Light," so these "Workers" are commanded to "let light be," to create a "green flowery World" that recovers the idyll of "unabated bounty" lost to enchantment in the opening paragraph of *Past and Present* (*SR*, 197; *PP*, 293–94, 7).

Past and Present succeeds where *Chartism* had failed because it does not attempt to frame its argument within the discourse of political economy but employs the rhetoric of religion to create an opposing discourse of value. Rather than simply providing a critique of contemporary society, Carlyle is able to create a vision of an alternative social order. He understood that his audience had allowed its religious beliefs to be separated from its everyday life in the world of industry, and *Past and Present* was his most effective piece of social criticism precisely because it created a powerful and relatively coherent ethical discourse that drew on the religious rhetoric with which his audience was familiar and applied it to the circumstances of their everyday lives.

Yet *Past and Present* only partially succeeds in reuniting the domains of religion and economy, for it envisions an escape from the commercial world into the transcendental idyll. It succeeds in part by making ethical discourse more powerful than the discourse of economy, but it remains powerful only in its visionary mode. At those moments when Carlyle presents his vision as a social and historical process, he turns to political force rather than religious belief in order to achieve the transcendental idyll.

Past and Present privileges material production over cultural production, the "done Work" over the "spoken Word" (160). Whereas in

Carlyle's earlier writings cultural myths had been the means through which action was infused with a transcendental moral order, now belief becomes posterior to, an efflorescence of, activity directed by the transcendent. The "old Epics" written on paper are no "longer possible," so the English epic must be "written on the Earth's surface" (293, 159; see 176; *CME*, 4:171–72). When Carlyle refers ambiguously to "[t]his English Land," the connotations of nation and culture elide with the connotations of physical land and agriculture (134). Instead of an expression of belief that transfuses the world and makes it an idyll, the idyll is a product of labor that literally builds a "green flowery world." Only through labor, he wrote elsewhere, could one find "salvation" (Faulkner, 157).

Throughout *Past and Present* and Carlyle's later writings, land reclamation and agriculture are the privileged forms of labor, coterminous with the aboriginal creative act, God's creation of the world in Genesis (esp. Gen. 1:9–11). The parallel with Genesis suggests that labor as creative activity continues the process through which the material world is infused with the transcendental order (see *PP*, 134–35). In the chapter entitled "Labour," Carlyle typically represents work as the transformation of a "pestilential swamp" where land and water mingle in "a green fruitful meadow with its clear-flowing stream" (197). These metaphors imply that the productions of agricultural labor—arable land—are permanent, while the productions of cultural labor—religious or literary texts—are ephemeral.

Carlyle's representations of the "Captain of Industry" owe a great deal to his enthusiasm for the men who were leading "poor starving drudges" out to found new colonies, to settle new lands (*CL*, 9:395). His support for emigration and colonization projects in *Chartism* and *Past and Present* is intimately linked to his vision of creation as the colonization of wasteland. Drawing on his depiction of creative work as bridge-building, he describes emigration as a "bridge" to the new world, a bridge that functions as a link between the earthly and the transcendental (*PP*, 263; see *CL*, 9:97). His writings distinguish two types of emigration, the transformation of wasteland into a paradise and the discovery of an El Dorado at the end of one's journey. The former is preferable because the process of seeking the idyll, labor, creates the idyll, whereas, in the latter case, the process of journeying only serves to defer achievement of that goal. Teufelsdröckh, like Goethe's Lothario, discovers that the search for the already achieved idyll never ends because one journeys endlessly from one illusory idyll to another. Discovering that their "America" is "here or nowhere," both turn to the creation of the idyll by working at "the duty which is nearest" (*SR*, 196; see *WM*, 2:11). Carlyle, who was increasingly inclined to associate writing with the endless search for the established El Dorado, contemplated going out himself to produce "bread" in one of the "waste places of . . . [the] Earth" rather than continuing the fruitless labor of writing (*CL*, 9:395; see 6:372–73, 8:14).[36]

However, Carlyle's depiction of the physical struggle of laborers who work to make land arable becomes subtly transformed into an argument for physically coercing laborers to engage in this activity. The shift from cultural to agricultural production in *Past and Present*, like the shift from belief to the law, entails a transition from compelling belief to compelling obedience. So long as Carlyle employs the metaphor of battle only to depict the struggle of the nation as a whole to create social order, it does not imply coercion or compulsion, but when he treats it more literally as the conquest of new lands, he begins to legitimate imperialist suppression and the very commercial motivations he intended to exclude.[37] Captains of industry not only turn wasteland into fertile pasture, but may force others to join them in the task (267). As Carlyle's metaphors make clear, he conceives of the captains of industry primarily as military captains fighting "the one true war" against social "anarchy" (271; see 270–72). Like critics of the new order from Coleridge to Tennyson, he insists that the apparent prosperity of the nation conceals the negation of a just social order, the reality of social warfare in which commerce cries, "Peace, Peace, where there is no Peace."[38] In this role, they fight not only against the primordial chaos of the land but the anarchy of humanity, "Organizing Labour" in order to subdue the "bewildering mob" into "a firm regimented mass" (272). The captain is a "Brave Sea-*captain*" like Christopher Columbus who "sternly repress[es]" his mutinous crew in order to discover an idyllic America, or an architect (recall the masonry metaphor) like Christopher Wren who organizes "mutinous masons and Irish hodmen" (199, 198; emphasis added). In the final analysis, the captain of industry does not resemble the medieval cleric Abbot Samson so much as the Puritan general Oliver Cromwell, whom Carlyle was to call "a strong great Captain" (*OCLS*, 4:173). One can see in retrospect that even Samson's success depended on the use of force; rowdy knights and recalcitrant monks obeyed him not because they shared his beliefs, but because he threatened them with "bolts" of "excommunication" (*PP*, 104).

Samson and the captains must use coercion because they, like the heroes who succeed Odin, are belated. Although Samson is a man of action, a builder of churches, he cannot duplicate the creative act of St. Edmund whose "Ideal . . . raised a Monastery"; he does not create a new idyll, he merely rebuilds an existing one (61, 63, 121). St. Edmund belongs to the "Beginnings," the timeless era before history began; by the time Samson arrives, the ideal that St. Edmund initially realized is buried under three centuries of history (131–36). Samson pulls the monastery back toward its beginnings, but he cannot fully escape history. The belated hero, unable to compel belief, must use force to compel obedience.

Carlyle represents through Samson his own feelings of belatedness, his anxiety that he can achieve nothing. Samson can at least build churches; Carlyle can only write books. Although Samson seems to spend more time building churches than religious faith, he at least shares his faith with the monks he guides. Carlyle can only imagine a communal ethos in his vision of the future; for the moment, there is no shared belief. Furthermore, he is uncertain about his power to shape the future. On the one hand, he imagines that, by becoming "an actual instead of a virtual Priesthood," men of letters can play a role in the recovery of belief; on the other hand, the future he imagines is one in which one must give up writing and begin to act (289).[39] While he is struggling to make writing a form of action, to prod his contemporaries into creating the future envisioned in the conclusion of *Past and Present*, he is aware that his book can only represent, not produce, that revolutionary change: "[I]t were fond imagination to expect that any preaching of mine could abate Mammonism; that Bobus of Houndsditch will love his guineas less, or his poor soul more, for any preaching of mine!" (290). Carlyle fears that instead of producing action, *Past and Present* might only be deferring it. Paradoxically, the idyll in which one rests from labor can only be created by labor. Like Samson, who can never completely recover the idyll he seeks to restore and so can never "rest," Carlyle needs to "work to keep [his] heart at rest" (*PP*, 103; *LL*, 1:182; emphasis added). Although he persistently advises his readers to give up writing and frequently speaks of giving it up himself, his own writings compel him to continue, each word calling for the production of another: "There seems no use in *living*," he wrote his brother, "if it be not writing, or preparing to write" (*CL*, 11:163).

Revolution in Search of Authority

In early 1844, when Carlyle determined on the expedient of editing Cromwell's letters and speeches and abandoned his attempt to write a history, he persisted in his intention of making *Oliver Cromwell's Letters and Speeches* a rewriting of *The French Revolution* in which revolution would recover rather than destroy authority. In *The French Revolution*, the narrative of increasing anarchy undermined the narrative in which the revolutionaries were striving to create a new social order by writing a constitution; in *Oliver Cromwell's Letters and Speeches*, Carlyle attempted, without success, to make the narrative in which Cromwell produces order dominate the narrative of increasing anarchy. The *Letters and Speeches* also persists with the dual purpose of rehabilitating Cromwell's reputation and bringing him back to life to reform nineteenth-century England; yet, while an edition of letters and speeches did succeed in altering the public's perception of Cromwell, it worked against the aim of bringing him back to life (see Frith, I:xxxiii; Abbott, 173–74). The Cromwell whose reputation Carlyle restored remained the Cromwell of the past.

The idea that the Puritans had sought to create a theocratic idyll dominated Carlyle's conception of the Puritan revolution from the beginning of his studies. Whereas the French Revolution had been the unleashing of anarchic forces that destroy the law, the Puritan revolution was the "attempt to bring the Divine Law of the Bible into actual practice in men's affairs on the Earth" (*OCLS*, 2:169). "The Theocracy which John Knox in his pulpit might dream of as a 'devout imagination,'" Carlyle wrote in *On Heroes and Hero-Worship*, Cromwell "dared to consider as capable of being *realised*" (226). The French Revolution was led by atheists who sought to establish democracy according to the gospel of Jean-Jacques Rousseau; the Puritan revolution was led by believers who sought to create a theocracy according to the gospel of Jesus Christ (*OCLS*, 1:266). The Puritans sought the ideal union of church and state, making the polity an "emblem" of the transcendental, so "That England should all become a Church" (1:82). Or, as he put it in one manuscript, "Church and State are Theory and Practice. Church is our Theorem of the invisible Eternity, wherein all that we name world in our earthly dialects, all from royal mantles to tinkers' aprons, seems but as an emblematic shadow" (*HS*, 275–76; see also *OCLS*, 1:81–82, 3:73–74, 308).

Cromwell, the king that Mirabeau might have been, possesses the authority to create this theocratic idyll. He shares with James Carlyle the ability to build and create, to speak and act meaningfully. Whereas the French fail in the attempt to "build" a new society by writing a constitution, Cromwell, an Orphic "melodious Worker" who makes "the stones, rocks, and big blocks dance into figures, into domed cities," successfully "buil[ds] together" a Puritan society (2:226–27, 4:207). Instead of making a constitution like the French, the Puritans let "search be made, Whether there is any King, *Könning*, Can-ning, or Supremely Able-Man that you can fall in with" (3:81). Cromwell is a "Tower" and his inauguration the "topstone"—recall the toppling "top-paper" of the failed French constitution—of the new social order (4:196, 124). Convinced that Cromwell's "practical contact with the Highest was a fact," Carlyle insists throughout the *Letters and Speeches* that his every action—his victories in battle, the execution of Charles I, even the massacres at Drogheda and Wexford—was a manifestation of the divine will: "From Naseby downwards, God, in the battle-whirlwind, seemed to speak and witness very audibly" (1:395, n. 1; see 1:148, 336, 412, 2:52, 3:46; *NL*, 1:314).

Yet the Puritan revolution follows the same course as the French Revolution, and Carlyle cannot help comparing them. Like the French, the English feel imprisoned, "pent within old limits" of "*untrue* Forms," and so rebel against and execute a king who is a "Solecism Incarnate" (*HS*, 268–69; *HHW*, 205; *FR*, 1:22; see *OCLS*, 2:245). Having destroyed royal authority, they inevitably become "sansculottic" and anarchic (e.g., *OCLS*, 3:224; see 1:290–91). In revolutionary France every man feels he is a king; in England there is danger of "every man making himself a Minister and Preacher" (*FR*, 3:40; *OCLS*, 3:120). The Barebones Parliament is England's "Assembly of Notables," the First Protectorate Parliament, like the Constituent Assembly, becomes occupied with "Constitution-building," and the "Agreement of the People" is little more than a "Bentham-Sieyes Constitution" (*OCLS*, 3:41, 156, 2:29; see 25). This era, too, is a "Paper Age," producing "tons of printed paper" (1:290). Instead of being united in Cromwell's theocracy, the nation is fragmented and thrown into civil war, a "Babel" of conflicting parties in which "Every man's hand" is "against his brother" (4:86, 3:108). Just as the last two volumes of *The French Revolution* depict the French nation drawn into the vortices of anarchy, so the latter two-thirds of *Oliver Cromwell's Letters and Speeches* depicts England threatened by "Abysses" and "black chaotic whirlwinds," the "Hydra" of anarchy proving just as indestructible as sansculottism (1:318, 3:224, 260).

If Cromwell succeeds in creating order, he does so not by founding order on a shared set of beliefs but by employing force. Carlyle argues that the people obey Cromwell's orders because they believe he is right, but he frequently finds himself justifying Cromwell's arbitrary use of power (e.g., 3:40, 4:15–18). He argues, for example, that Cromwell is right to "repress" the Scots and "bind" them "in tight manacles" because they are creating anarchic "confusion" (2:170). But England is so far from consensus that Cromwell not only "coerce[s]" royalists and levelers, he even "eject[s]" Puritan ministers who dissent from his views (3:201). Far from creating a paradisal theocracy in which social order reflects transcendental justice, Cromwell must struggle merely to keep the lid on anarchy.

In this regard, Cromwell resembles Dr. Francia, the Paraguayan dictator that Carlyle had defended in an essay written shortly after he completed *Past and Present* in 1843 and while he was still having difficulties with the Cromwell project. His representation of Francia transforms the career of the man of letters into that of the king by shifting the emphasis from culture and belief to power and the law. Like Carlyle, Francia contemplates a religious vocation, develops hypochondria (a trait shared with Cromwell as well), enters the university, is influenced by the *philosophes,* quarrels with his father, and shifts his studies to the law. When, soon after the French Revolution, a rebellion tumbles Paraguay into anarchy, he establishes himself as "king" in order to restore social order and ensure that justice is done (*CME,* 4:305). Placing a high value on work, like all of Carlyle's heroes, Francia orders the capital city to be rebuilt. Yet Francia's success is clearly indebted to the harsh measures he employs to repress the populace. Anticipating his defense of Cromwell's Irish massacres, Carlyle endeavors to explain away Francia's "reign of terror" as a "reign of rigour," but the scaffold Francia raises to warn the people of the cost of disobedience both reminds us that the French "reign of Terror" employed the same menace and reveals that the people must be coerced (*CME,* 4:302). Carlyle makes no pretense that Francia compels belief; he admires him only because he restores order (see Collmer, Weaver).

Because only Cromwell's personal power sustains the Protectorate, it cannot survive in his absence. Like Francia and the French, he does not create a cultural consensus that produces order but merely represses disorder. Consequently, with his death, England soon falls "into *Kinglessness*, what we call Anarchy" (4:183; see 173). Rather than providing an alternative to the French Revolution, the Puritan revolution, as Carlyle himself acknowledges, inaugurated the era of revolutionary anarchy that would not end until the process initiated by Cromwell was complete.[40]

Carlyle made a hero of Cromwell by choosing a form, the edition of letters and speeches, that privileges Cromwell's voice, allowing it to dominate and silence the competing voices of revolution. Cromwell remains a hero for Carlyle because he at least made an attempt to create a theocratic idyll and because he managed to hold off anarchy so long as he lived. Whereas the anarchy of the French Revolution had been characterized by the multiple voices of the revolutionary factions, Carlyle's conception of the Puritan era called for the subsumption of the multifarious voices of the seventeenth century into the single voice of Cromwell, a Cromwell Carlyle hoped to invoke in order to restore unity to the fragmented culture of his own century.

The narrative technique of *Oliver Cromwell's Letters and Speeches* reflects this monologic vision of Puritan culture. Whereas *The French Revolution* had used the first-person plural to represent the variety of historical actors, and Carlyle's Cromwell manuscripts sometimes suggest the possibility of using lively "dialogues," nothing like this appears in the final text of the *Letters and Speeches*.[41] When Carlyle does use the first-person technique, it almost invariably represents the privileged voices of Cromwell or the Puritans; instead of representing a debate among competing factions, it asserts the dominance of the Puritan ethos and manifests the identification between Carlyle and Cromwell.[42]

The letters and speeches format also reinforces Carlyle's contention that Cromwell's language, like James Carlyle's, had "a meaning in it" (2:53). Carlyle's insistence that Cromwell's every word had value led him to include every letter no matter how trivial, even to accept as genuine the forgeries of William Squire (see Ryals). The narrator of *The French Revolution* had to interpret dry-as-dust documents, to decide which provided clues to the meaning of the revolution and which were mere waste paper. The narrator of *Oliver Cromwell's Letters and Speeches* needs only to put Cromwell's letters and speeches in order, since Cromwell's meaningful words require no interpretation. Carlyle forsakes the role of historical interpreter and becomes a mere "Pious Editor," even subordinating his own words by having them printed in smaller type than that used for Cromwell's letters and speeches.[43]

Yet Carlyle seems to grow increasingly restless in the role of hero-worshipping editor, and we soon find him drawing our attention from Cromwell's words to his own. Carlyle's commentaries are meant to provide a narrative context that links together the sequence of letters; it is therefore necessarily subordinate to them. Through about one-sixth of the work he stays with this plan, but then he suddenly breaks in to request that the reader defer reading Cromwell's letters in order to read an "Extract from a work still in Manuscript" (1:258). The work Carlyle quotes is, of course, his own abandoned history of the civil wars. The extract is immediately set apart from the preceding narrative by its vivid metaphor and lively syntax, its playfulness (e.g., a pun on "Divines" and "Dry-Vines"), and its representation of the voices of "London City" and "the Army." It functions as a metacommentary that focuses on Carlyle's own concerns rather than glossing Cromwell's texts. From this point forward, Carlyle's distinctive voice begins to emerge, and passages like this one appear with increasing frequency (e.g., 1:264–65, 2:226–27, 3:70–72, 83–84, 111, n. 1).

Carlyle's increasing discomfort with the role of editor becomes most conspicuous in his handling of Cromwell's speeches. The first half of the work is fairly equally divided between Cromwell's letters, which are usually less than a page long, and Carlyle's linking narrative. The speeches, many of which run to thirty or forty pages, threaten to silence Carlyle for long stretches of time in the latter half of the book, but he finds a means to introduce himself even in the midst of them. In his introduction to the second speech, he advises us that in order to make the speeches more accessible to his modern audience he has "with reluctance, admitted from the latest of the Commentators a few annotations" (3:105). The latest of the Commentators is, once again, Carlyle. What is most striking about these "annotations" is that they do not appear as footnotes but as comments interpolated within the texts of the speeches. Although square brackets set them off from the text, the comments are emphatically italicized. Whereas the use of reduced-size type subordinated his commentary to the letters, this typographical convention makes every comment stand out on the page.

Since the comments appear in the body of the text, the reader can hardly ignore them; instead of making us pay greater attention to Cromwell, they keep drawing our attention to the narrator. The interpolations are in part a means to bring the speeches to life by creating the fiction of an audience listening to and observing Cromwell in the here and now. The most common are audience reactions, cries of "Hear!" "Yea!" "Alas!" "So!" and "Hum-m-m!"; others function as stage directions, describing the gestures and emotions of the crowd and Cromwell himself—one, for example, depicts him "looking up, with a mournful toss of the head" (3:124; see 106–26). Yet the reader cannot but be aware that if Cromwell seems to come to life it is not through his own words—which remain dry and wooden—but through the words Carlyle has added to the text of his speeches.[44] Only about a third of the interpolations are genuine glosses that might help the reader understand what Cromwell is saying, and even these often displace Cromwell's statements rather than simply explain them. These interpolations frequently interrupt Cromwell in mid-sentence, a practice hardly calculated to help us follow the course of his arguments (e.g., 3:113–14, 115–16, 119). Finally, Carlyle's admiration for Cromwell and his insistence that his speech is "meaningful" does not prevent him from losing patience at times with his hobbyhorses—"The justifying of the Spanish War is a great point with his Highness!"—or making fun of his more awkward locutions—"I am a man standing in the Place I am in [*Clearly, your Highness*]" (3:277, 4:58; see 3:118–19). Rather than encouraging readers to worship at the feet of the Puritan hero, such comments invite them to assume a position of bemused detachment, of the nineteenth century condescending to the seventeenth.

Carlyle has another difficulty in his efforts to make Cromwell's career a living epic. In *The French Revolution*, as in *Past and Present*, he had discovered the fundamental belief of the era by interpreting its everyday activities, but although his manuscripts represent him as seeking a symbolic structure for the history, the *Letters and Speeches* are almost totally devoid of symbolic interpretation. In part, Carlyle's difficulties arose because his thesis differed from that of *The French Revolution*. In the latter, symbols proliferated in proportion to the diversity of human activities, but in the history of the Puritans Carlyle sought symbols that manifested the unified divine will. The divine will was manifested in battle; yet, apart from Cromwell's assertion that this was so, the history of the battles themselves contained nothing to distinguish them from the battles of any other war. Carlyle could find no symbolic episodes like the mutiny at Nancy or the storming of the Bastille.

The one episode that seemed to possess some symbolic resonance was the episode of Jenny Geddes, and Carlyle attempted on several occasions to elaborate it into a central episode of his history. The episode revolved around the legend that the pious Jenny Geddes had flung a stool at the dean of St. Giles when Archbishop Laud attempted to introduce the Anglican prayer book into the services of the Church of Scotland. Carlyle's manuscripts suggest that he wanted to portray this incident, which, according to the story, set off riots throughout Edinburgh, as the *"first* stroke in an infinite bout" that "spread . . . over Edinburgh, over broad Scotland at large" and was symbolic of *"latter* strokes" like those which beheaded Charles I (*CL*, 11:36, 13:74; *HS*, 10). As early as February 1839, when he first began his Cromwell studies, Carlyle had depicted Geddes as an epic "heroine," first the Iphigenia, then the Helen of the civil wars (*CL*, 11:36; *OCLS*, 1:97).[45] But he soon found that no document contemporary with the Edinburgh riot mentioned Geddes, indeed, that the legend had not appeared until several decades after the event; its unique mythic potential derived from the fact that it really was myth, that there was little historical basis for it.[46] In the end, Carlyle relegated it to a brief passage in the introduction to the *Letters and Speeches* (1:96–97). He could not risk founding his epic on an event that might never have taken place; but neither could he discover any historical event that offered the same symbolic potential.

Carlyle's decision simply to edit the letters and speeches signaled his abandonment of the search for the symbolic; indeed, the letters and speeches format worked against the discovery of the symbolic. Whereas the narrator-editors of *Sartor Resartus*, *The French Revolution*, and *Past and Present* feel free to subordinate chronology in order to arrange material symbolically, the strict chronological arrangement of the letters and speeches limits the pious Editor's ability to discover symbols or present the history of the civil wars in symbolic terms. Confining himself to the events of Cromwell's career as exhibited in the letters, he is forced to exclude potentially symbolic material. For example, in *The French Revolution*, Carlyle devotes an entire book, about fifty pages, to the trial and execution of Louis XVI, while the trial and execution of Charles I in the *Letters and Speeches* merits only half a dozen pages. His manuscripts, especially *Historical Sketches*, are rich in the kind of anecdotal history in which he liked to read the signs of the times—Guy Fawkes's gunpowder plot, duelling, the burning of the playhouse in Drury Lane, the Book of Sports, and so on—but he finally excluded almost all this material because he could not find a way to relate it to the life of Cromwell. Whereas Carlyle's earlier works had built up complex vocabularies of imagery, trope, and allusion through which to convey his symbolic reading of events (for example, the clothing imagery and the fictional framework of *Sartor Resartus*; the imagery of the vortex and fire, the Homeric allusions, and the personifications of *The French Revolution*; the figure of the Irish widow, the contrast between the monastery of St. Edmund and the St. Ives workhouse, and the image of the "cash-nexus" in *Past and Present*), *Oliver Cromwell's Letters and Speeches* simply lacks a coherent system of signs through which to present a symbolic reading of the civil wars.

Carlyle closely identified the Puritans and the Scottish rebels with his own ancestors and had long regarded them as spiritual "fathers" (e.g., 1:80, 3:211, 4:208). His attempt to recuperate the idyll of Puritanism was yet another attempt to recover the idyll lost with the death of his father and to author a new myth for the nineteenth century. Like the Fifth Monarchists, he longed for an apocalyptic "Monarchy of Jesus Christ," and, like Smelfungus in the *Historical Sketches*, he hoped to "restore" the past in such a way that it would "never . . . be lost more" (*OCLS*, 3:113; *HS*, 38). Having taken as his goal nothing less than the completion of the revolution Cromwell had begun, he could not but feel that he had failed.

Carlyle complained in the introduction to the *Letters and Speeches* that, while the English people had consummated the "*epic*" act of "Choosing their King," the history of English heroism remained unuttered, imprisoned in the "labyrinth . . . that we call Human History" (4:37, 1:7). Yet, like his literary predecessors, Carlyle also failed to transform the "dead indescribable *Cromwelliad*" into a "living *Iliad*" (1:5). In part, he failed because he could not bring himself to believe in a "dialect" as "obsolete" as Odin's and Dante's; Puritanism, he concluded, was not a "Complete Theory of this immense Universe; no, only a part thereof!" (2:53, 4:184). In part, he failed because his researches demonstrated that Cromwell's theocratic idyll had never existed, that contrary to escaping time and history, Cromwell and the

Puritans had inaugurated the era of revolution. The irony of the *Letters and Speeches* is that it consists entirely of written documents, of Cromwell's words; like Teufelsdröckh, Samson, and Carlyle himself, Cromwell speaks endlessly but earns no rest other than the rest of death (3:107, 124). In the three years following the publication of *Cromwell*, Carlyle's remaining hope that he might create a Cromwell to bring order and justice to England faded away. The powerlessness of writing never seemed more apparent. When Cromwell could not persuade the opposition to agree with him, he could use force to keep them in order; when Carlyle failed to persuade his contemporaries to accept a new Cromwell, the only force he could resort to was the force of angry words.

From the "Irish Question" to "The Nigger Question"[47]

When Carlyle finished seeing the first edition of *Oliver Cromwell's Letters and Speeches* through the press in August 1845, it seemed for a short while that he had indeed succeeded in bringing Cromwell to life. Carlyle had almost certainly been thinking of his own time when he wrote in the *Letters and Speeches* that "to them, and to us, there can only one thing be done: search be made, Whether there is any King, *Könning*, Canning, or Supremely Able-Man that you can fall in with" (2:286). Peel now seemed ready to fill that role by abrogating the Corn Laws in fulfillment of the prophecy Carlyle had made in 1841. But the politics of the nineteenth century would not permit Peel to make himself either king or lord protector, and just six months after finishing *Cromwell*, Carlyle felt that he must act on his own to release "imprisoned" heroism (see *LDP*, 335).

To reinforce the symbolic relationship between Peel and Cromwell and to encourage Peel to emulate Cromwell, Carlyle sent him a copy of the second edition of the *Letters and Speeches* in May 1846, the month the Corn Laws were repealed. The letter that accompanied his book encouraged Peel to assume the role of hero, to act forcefully rather than waste his time with parliamentary speech-making (*LL*, 1:402–3; see Seigel, "Carlyle and Peel").[48] Carlyle would have liked to see Peel deal with Parliament as Cromwell had. In spite of their loyalty to Cromwell and the Puritan cause, Cromwell's parliaments, not unlike the reform parliaments of the 1840s, proved unable to act because they became enmeshed in debate. Instead of arguing with his deadlocked parliaments, Cromwell took action, simply dissolving them (3:194, 4:179–80). Yet Peel could not even maintain discipline in his own party, let alone dissolve Parliament and rule England through major-generals. On the contrary, repeal of the Corn Laws brought a swift end to his ministry and virtually ended his political career. Although Carlyle hoped that Peel would return to power, an aim that *Latter-Day Pamphlets* was partly intended to effect, he could not help but see in Peel's fall the rejection of his own political program.

Carlyle soon discovered that, although readers were impressed and persuaded by his representation of the seventeenth-century Cromwell, they had no desire for a Cromwell of their own. Robert Vaughn's notice in the *British Quarterly Review* was typical. He praised Carlyle's scholarly ability and was persuaded that Cromwell's religious piety was sincere, but he disparaged Carlyle's "endless lamentation over modern degeneracy" as well as "his prostrate adoration before the real or imaginary greatness of bygone days," and treated the attempt to make Cromwell live for the nineteenth century—for Carlyle the sole purpose of the book—as an irrelevant deviation from history (Seigel, *Critical Heritage*, 271). Carlyle concluded that "Nobody on the whole '*believes* my report.' The friendliest reviewers, I can see, regard me as a wonderful athlete, a ropedancer whose perilous somersets it is worth sixpence . . . to *see;* or at most I seem to them a desperate half mad, if usefullish fireman, rushing along the ridge tiles in a frightful manner to quench the burning chimney. Not one of them all can or will *do* the least to help me" (*LL*, 1:452–53). The public now respected Cromwell, but, as he was to reflect bitterly in "Hudson's Statue," it did not worship him.

If, in the absence of Peel, Carlyle were to play the role of Cromwell, he would need once again to seek a means of turning writing into action. The rhetoric he employed in "The Negro/Nigger Question" and *Latter-Day Pamphlets* seeks to coerce and attack rather than persuade and convert his audience. In the process of developing this rhetoric, he also transformed what was originally a plan for a sympathetic analysis of the "Irish Question" into the antagonistic "Negro/Nigger Question" and the apocalyptic *Latter-Day Pamphlets*.

The "Irish Question," particularly the issue of repeal of the union between England and Ireland, was a major issue in the 1840s. From the time of *Sartor Resartus*, in which he represented the poor as Irish peasants, to 1848, when he lamented the influx of indigents driven out of Ireland by irresponsible landlords, Carlyle had considered the condition of Ireland a key to understanding the condition of England (*SR*, 283–84; Marrs, 668). In spite of the fact that he held the Irish aristocracy responsible for the poverty of Ireland, he opposed the repeal of the union of England and Ireland that would pave the way for Irish self-determination.[49] As usual, he forged a position between the two parties. In 1845, he had become acquainted with several leaders of the Young Ireland movement, visiting them in Ireland in 1846. In 1849, he offended the government, which also opposed repeal, by touring Ireland with Gavan Duffy, an Irish nationalist who remained his lifelong friend. But, during the same tour, he privately depicted Duffy's associates as "canaille" (Bliss, 250). At first he argued, as he had in *Past and Present*, that the problem was not essentially political or economic, but moral: "For it is want of sense and honesty, not want of potatoes, that we now suffer under," he wrote in 1847, "all the yearly potatoes of the British Empire are supposed to be worth some 20, or 25 or 30 millions; and all the yearly *harvest* of the British Empire . . . must be between 200 and 300 millions:—a Nation, one would say, that reaped such a harvest (good all of it, except the potatoes) last year, and had so many Manchester and other big Workshops going,—this Nation should not die for the loss of a few potatoes, if it had 'sense and honesty' in it!"[50] Yet he had lost hope that he could convert his contemporaries and restore to them the "moral sense" he had called for in *Past and Present*.

During 1846–47, Carlyle prepared himself to write a book on Ireland, but it was not until the revolutions of 1848 that he finally set to work in earnest.[51] No sooner had he heard the news of the first uprising on the Continent than he returned to his journal after a long period of silence to set down four possible writing projects, three of which were concerned with the condition of England: "Ireland: Spiritual Sketches," which would examine the misery of Ireland in terms of its spiritual history; "Exodus from Houndsditch," on the need to rid England of its old clothes (Houndsditch was the district where used clothing was sold), particularly institutional Christianity; and "The Scavenger Age," on the need to clean the metaphoric gutters of England as the "indispensable beginning of all" reform (*LL*, 1:455; Kaplan, 332). In March, he rejoiced to hear of the revolution in France, responding with jubilant letters to his friends and a newspaper article on the dethroned Louis-Philippe. At home, the Irish nationalists attempted an uprising, and Chartism, preparing its third and final petition, threatened violence. This time, he hoped, revolution, having completed the destruction of outworn authority, would discover a new Cromwell who would prove that the "righteous gods do still rule this earth."[52]

In April and May, he wrote a series of articles on Ireland that shocked and offended not only his Irish acquaintances but his old friend John Stuart Mill (see Tarr, "Carlyle and Henry M'Cormac"). He argued that repeal of the union of England and Ireland was another instance of the government abdicating its responsibility to govern, that what was needed was not less government but better government. No one could have been surprised that he opposed repeal; his arguments against it are entirely consistent with his previous writings. But what his friends were probably not prepared for was the tone of the articles, the strenuousness with which he insisted that "Eternal law," the "Law of the Universe," "the laws of fact," and "the inexorable gods" had decreed the unity of England and Ireland and laid upon England a "terrible job of labour," to create order in Ireland (Shepherd, 2:379, 380, 381, 383, 377).[53] Putting his paternalism at the service of imperialism, he argued that the Irish must either "become British," or—and here he certainly had his defense of Cromwell at Drogheda in mind—become "extinct; cut off by the inexorable gods" (383).

Mill immediately recognized the "new phasis" of Carlyle's writings. Whereas Carlyle had previously placed the blame for England's problems on the aristocracy, he now was arguing that the aristocracy alone could solve these problems: "Instead of telling of the sins and errors of England, and warning her of 'wrath to come,' as he has been wont to do, he preaches the divine Messiahship of England." Mill also recognized that Carlyle longed for a Cromwell to fill the messianic role, but objected that Lord Russell was no Cromwell and that the same England that had mismanaged the governing of Ireland for centuries seemed unlikely to succeed any better now (*Newspaper Writings*, 1096, 1098–99).[54] Mill could not have been expected to realize that Carlyle was calling for the return of Peel.

However, Carlyle's last remaining hope that the breakdown of government would permit a new Cromwell to emerge was crushed when it became clear in the summer of 1848 that the revolutions had failed. The French had replaced Louis Philippe not with a hero but with a conventional government. The crisis in Britain had not even been sufficient to unseat Russell, let alone provide an opening for Peel. Rather than heeding the demand for reform, Russell simply suppressed the opposition, jailing the Irish rebels, including Carlyle's friend Gavan Duffy, and the leaders of the Chartists.

In the spring of 1849, Carlyle decided that his ideas "might perhaps get nearer to some way of utterance if [he] were looking face to face upon the ruin and wretchedness that [was] prevalent" in Ireland (*LL*, 1:491). Although he had never been more desperate to address the problems of his era, he still could not decide how to approach them. As early as 1846, he was complaining, "I am at the bottom, and nothing is yet said!" and, three years later, that "a *Book* is sticking in my heart, which cannot get itself written at all; and till that be written there is no hope of peace or benefit for me anywhere" (Marrs, 635; Duffy, 135). He had produced a great deal of manuscript and the series of newspaper articles, but the feeling that he was getting nowhere oppressed him so much that he felt as if he had been utterly idle (*LL*, 1:436–37, 452; *LMSB*, 282; *RWE*, 437; Faulkner, 168, 169, 170). Yet although he felt that he "ought to go and . . . must go" to Ireland, he anticipated that he would not "find much new knowledge" there (*LL*, 1:491; see *NL*, 2:70). His anticipation was fulfilled, perhaps even desired. Although he considered Ireland "the notablest of all spots in the world at present," he found himself upon his return "farther from *speech* on any subject than ever" and never wrote the book on Ireland (Duffy, 135; *RWE*, 455).

The surviving manuscripts reveal Carlyle's inability to imagine constructive approaches to England's problems. While he had initially intended to analyze the Irish Question in terms of religious belief—in a series of "spiritual sketches"—he kept turning to the old problems: laissez-faire political and economic policy. He no longer could persuade himself that religious belief alone, or literature, would solve England's problems, and concluded that "Plugson," whom he had imagined converting in *Past and Present*, had gained "almost no insight into the laws of this universe whatever" ("Rakes," fol. 12).[55] "The Negro Question" and *Latter-Day Pamphlets* manifest Carlyle's despair at being unable to effect any meaningful change.

In November of 1849, still worried that what he had written thus far was "wrongish, every word" of it, but feeling that he needed to "give vent to" himself, Carlyle decided to proceed with publication of a series of pamphlets (*LL*, 2:24; *NL*, 2:86). Serial publication allowed him to go ahead with publication at a time when he still had not worked out a complete plan of the work. His original plan to publish twelve pamphlets suggests an attempt to give the work an epic structure, but although the desire to write a new epic was there, the vision was lacking. Even as he wrote the sixth pamphlet he still had no plan for a conclusion, and he abandoned the project after completing only eight.[56] Whereas *Past and Present* had moved toward a conclusion in which Carlyle imagined and represented the conversion of his audience, *Latter-Day Pamphlets* never reached a conclusion. Instead of attempting to create a community of fellow believers—as he had sought to do when he moved to London in 1834—he went on the attack against his contemporaries for failing to understand him. In part, he was angry because they had not understood the real message of *Oliver Cromwell's Letters and Speeches*; in part, he was venting on his audience his frustration at his inability to achieve something with his writing. He saw himself beset by a public that was determined to cause him pain and to keep him from writing, the only means he possessed "to defend [him]self against the world without, and keep it from overwhelming [him], as it often threatens to do" (*LL*, 1:476–77). "I mean to hurt nobody, I," he wrote a few months later, "and the hurt that others (involuntarily for most part) do me is incalculable. . . . It seems as if all things were combining against me to hinder any book or free deliverance of myself I might have in view at present" (*LL*, 1:483–84). In the *Latter-Day Pamphlets*, the speaker is not the prophet warning his audience of the day of reckoning to come, but the divine scourge itself, "rag[ing]" and "growl[ing]" at his audience, and running verbal "red-hot poker[s]" through its cherished beliefs (*LDP*, 315, 21; *NL*, 2:85).[57]

Whereas Carlyle represents the audience of *Past and Present* as morally inadequate but capable of discovering moral truth, he represents the audience of *Latter-Day Pamphlets* as permanently blinded, fools and "blockheads" (e.g., 265). In *Past and Present*, he creates at least the semblance of debate between his avatars and his audience; in *Latter-Day Pamphlets* he tends to cut off debate. While he employs once again a wide range of fictional personae, his handling of Quashee, the Duke of Trumps, the Hon. Hickory Buckskin, Duncan M'Pastehorn, Friend Heavyside, and Gathercoal is far more satirical and heavy-handed than the use of Plugson of Undershot or Friend Prudence in *Past and Present*. The Carlyle of *Latter-Day Pamphlets* hopes that "one in the thousand" will "see . . . what [he] see[s]" and "forgive" him for berating them, but he is never able to envision this moment as he had in *Past and Present*; he has despaired of converting Plugson (296). Although he reintroduces the captains of industry as an incipient aristocracy in the first pamphlet, he no longer addresses, or manifests any faith in, a specific class in which he hopes to find converts (35; see 24). Rather than imagining the industrial middle class as leaders who will reshape society, he imagines that some higher authority will have to "force" them "to coöperate" with the state and its "public Captains" (166).

The rhetorical strategy of these works is to test his audience in order to discover whether they belong to the elect and to drive away unbelievers. The altered relationship between Carlyle and his audience can be observed in "The Nigger Question," which he framed as a discourse delivered before a philanthropic audience dedicated to the abolition of slavery, the "UNIVERSAL ABOLITION-OF-PAIN ASSOCIATION." This speech is punctuated with representations of audience reactions modeled on the simulated audience responses Carlyle had interpolated into Cromwell's speeches. In the resulting metanarrative, the audience of the fictional speaker dwindles steadily until only a "small remnant"—suggestive of the "saving remnant of Israel"—remains to give assent to his doctrines (see August 21, 33).[58] If this is a reflection of Carlyle's recognition that "The Negro Question" and *Latter-Day Pamphlets* had driven away many of his faithful readers, it also reveals something about the technique of these works, in which the speaker does not seek to convert but to test his audience, to discover the saving remnant.

Unable to convert his contemporaries, Carlyle cut himself off from them, leaving himself a "minority of one" (*CME*, 4:348; see *HHW*, 61). In "dissent from all the world," he insisted that he could no longer be identified with or accepted by conventional parties, sects, and institutions, even the literary vehicles in which he had so often appeared (*LL*, 2:24). While in the 1830s he had been frustrated when editors refused to accept his writings, he now proudly claimed that "There is no Newspaper that can stand my articles, no *single* Newspaper that they would not blow the bottom out of in a short while!" (*LL*, 1:470).[59] Where he had once hoped to astonish all parties, he now wanted to alienate them: "All the twaddling sects of the country, from Swedenborgians to Jesuits, have for the last ten years been laying claim to 'T. Carlyle,' each for itself; and now they will all find that said 'T.'

belongs to a sect of his own, which is worthy of instant damnation"
(*NL*, 1:86–87). With *Latter-Day Pamphlets*, which cuts off speakers and
allows only Carlyle's own personae to speak, Carlyle locked himself up
once more in a world even more isolated than Craigenputtoch.

Carlyle's self-enclosure manifests itself in *Latter-Day Pamphlets* in the
reduction of the dialogue between the narrator and the many factions
of English society to a dialogue with himself. The principal audience is
the prime minister—Carlyle frequently addresses "your Lordship"—
yet the prime minister he imagines is ultimately himself. *Latter-Day
Pamphlets* envisions a prime minister modeled on Cromwell who will
reform "Downing Street" and regiment the nation. In addressing and
dramatizing the prime minister, Carlyle has in mind three figures: the
incumbent Russell, his predecessor Peel, and himself. He addresses
several appeals to Russell, but he has no desire to reform him. Russell,
he claims, has donned the "battle-harness" of Cromwell but does not
really intend to do battle against anarchy and will never be capable of
governing (123).[60] Russell should be turned out in favor of "the one
likely man or possible man to reform" Downing Street, "King" Peel
(92; see 97). Peel would reestablish hierarchy by animating "intelli-
gent circles" of followers through whom he would transmit his plans
for reform and establish social order. But, although Carlyle appears to
sustain some hope that Peel will return to office, his representation of
the Cromwellian prime minister has less to do with Peel's parliamentary initiatives than with his own fantasies about what he would do if
"they were to make [him] Cromwell of it all" (*CL*, 14:47).

Although *Latter-Day Pamphlets* is overtly an argument for making
Peel prime minister, it is more subtly an argument for a prime minister modeled on the Carlylean persona. Carlyle's identification with
Burns and his lament that the man of letters does not have a more
active career available to him, together with his argument that men like
Burns, who are "born king[s] of men" should not be excluded from
governing merely because they come from the "lowest and broadest
stratum of Society," become arguments in favor of his own eligibility
for public office (118). The speech by the prime minister that concludes the first pamphlet, "The Present Time," could never have been
uttered by Russell or Peel; it belongs entirely to the Carlyle who in-
dulges throughout the *Pamphlets* in imagining what he would do if he
"had a commonwealth to reform or to govern" (58). Not surprisingly,
a good deal of Cromwell is infused into this persona. When the prime

minister of this speech warns his audience of Irish paupers that, if they continue to disobey him, he will "admonish," "flog," and "if still in vain . . . shoot" them, he is repeating Cromwell's warning to the Irish at Drogheda: "Refuse to obey [the laws], I will not let you continue living" (*LDP*, 46; *OCLS*, 2:54).[61]

A number of critics have argued convincingly that, while Carlyle's social analyses remain much the same in *Latter-Day Pamphlets*, his rhetoric has changed (LaValley, 279–86; Levine, "Use and Abuse," 117–23; Goldberg, "A Universal 'howl,'" 138). Yet it would be wrong to stop with an analysis of the rhetoric of these works. Although in many regards Carlyle's arguments do remain the same, their emphasis has shifted in significant ways. What made and makes these works offensive is that changes in the nature of his analyses of freedom, of the necessity of work, and of social responsibility shift the blame for social problems from the ruling classes to the working class, and in the process resort to racial stereotyping. Although his conception of industrial regiments, which would "regenerate" society and produce a theocratic "*Civitas Dei*," is an extention of the idea of building a "green flowery world" with which he had concluded *Past and Present*, it shifts the source of the labor from the ruling class—the captains—to the poverty-stricken laboring class (159, 166).[62] The shift in his military metaphors is telling. In *Past and Present*, where he was concerned with "captains of industry," he attacked and sought to reform the ruling classes. In *Latter-Day Pamphlets*, where he proposes empressing the un-employed in "Industrial Regiments," he attacks and seeks to control the poor. Because he would force all able-bodied paupers to enlist, his proposal for industrial regiments, which would impose a hierarchical military order on industry, is in effect a proposal for establishing slavery in England (41–43). It is, in fact, of a piece with his arguments against abolition in "The Negro/Nigger Question."

"The Negro/Nigger Question" takes up the discourse of the debate on the nature of freedom touched off by the abolition movement. At the center of this debate, which began in the 1770s and developed further in the early nineteenth century, was the analogy between slaves and factory workers widely used both by defenders of slavery and critics of industry.[63] Political economists, who defined freedom in strictly economic terms as the freedom to buy and sell one's labor in the marketplace, generally regarded abolition of slavery as an extension of laissez-faire principle. Critics of the laissez-faire marketplace, and of industry in particular, challenged this notion of freedom, arguing that slaves were better off than the majority of English laborers, who were slaves of necessity, as the simple need to survive deprived them of their theoretical freedom to seek better employment. Carlyle, like his predecessors in this debate, often gives an ironic intonation to the word *free* by putting it in quotation marks, implying that the freedom offered by emancipation is only nominal, that it would not free slaves from the hardships of human existence (*LDP*, 24, 40).

The slaves-of-necessity argument was used by anti-abolitionists to argue that slavery was no different than industrial labor, and by critics of industry, like Coleridge, to argue that slavery should be abolished and industrial capitalism regulated. Both Coleridge and Carlyle attempted to define freedom in ethical rather than economic terms, but they could do no better than claim that freedom was "best expressed and enforced through a traditional hierarchy of social relationships that defined one's 'duty'" (Gallagher, 18). The "free man," Carlyle writes, "is he who is *loyal* to the Laws of this Universe" (*LDP*, 251). When Carlyle supported slavery, he was not really departing from Coleridge's position but admitting more frankly that the hierarchical social order they both desired, harkening back as it did to medieval serfdom, entailed a form of slavery. He thus inverts Coleridge, arguing, in effect, that slavery should be extended to the British working class.

Latter-Day Pamphlets and "The Nigger Question" represent the relationship between masters and laborers through the metaphor of farmers and horses, a transformation of the metaphor of horse and halter— representing rebellion and authority—that Carlyle had developed in the 1830s. When, in *Sartor Resartus*, the young *sansculotte* Teufelsdröckh rejects the constraints of the law, he is depicted as a "colt" who breaks off his "neck-halter"; and, in *The French Revolution*, the French people are depicted as "gin-horses" who rear up when threatened with the "whip" (*SR*, 121; *FR*, 1:5). In *Sartor Resartus*, Carlyle also points out that whereas a manufacturer will lay off his workers and let them starve during a slack season, horse owners would never think of neglecting their horses just because they have no work for them (230). In *Chartism* and *Past and Present*, Carlyle combined the two figures to suggest that treating horses according to the principles of laissez-faire—abandoning them to survive through the winter when one has no work for them—would lead to a horse rebellion, horses "leaping fences" and "eating foreign property" (*CME*, 4:142, 158; *PP*, 27; see 277). Horses would be justified in rebelling because they need to eat, he implies, but rebellion is not necessary if masters do their duty. In *Latter-Day Pamphlets*, and later in "The Nigger Question," he appears much less concerned that the horses might eventually starve than that they refuse to work for Farmer Hodge and are "wasting the seedfields of the world" (*LDP*, 27). The analogy is no longer an argument against laissez-faire so much as an extension of the proslavery argument against the emancipation of slaves. Whereas the Carlyle of 1830, the struggling author, had identified with the rebellious horse, the Carlyle of 1850 identifies with the agrarian capitalist.[64]

Carlyle's desire to rationalize his proposal for industrial regiments led him to take up positions that contradicted his critique of political economy. The situation in the West Indies provided the opportunity to shift the focus of his analysis. He had long argued that the English poor were starving because employers failed to provide for them in times of dearth when employment was not available, but the situation in the Indies was different. The West Indians were refusing the work offered them because they preferred to work for themselves, to establish their own subsistence economy. Carlyle argues that they are refusing the only real work available to them, that their work, as opposed to that done by English planters, is not productive: "the gods wish beside pumpkins, that spices and *valuable* products be grown," and so the English have produced "fruit spicy and *commercial*, fruit spiritual and celestial" (*CME*, 4:375, 373; emphasis added). But, as Mill immediately perceived, Carlyle's argument relies upon the assumption that spices and sugar are more valuable because they are "commercial," because they have value in the capitalist economy, a startling contradiction of his belief that value cannot be defined in economic terms (*Essays on Equality*, 90, 92).[65]

Carlyle's advocacy of forced labor—in the guise of prime minister he warns the idle Irish that he will make them work—similarly reverses his earlier critiques of the political economists (*LDP*, 44). Whereas he had once argued that the poor were forced by circumstances (e.g., that no work was available) to go on relief, in 1849 he complains that the "one or two thousand great hulks of men lying piled up within brick walls" of the workhouse in Killarney simply refuse to work (*RIJ*, 77; see 175–76). But, once again, work has become allied to capitalist production—his industrial regiments produce "green crops, and fresh butter and milk and beef without limit"—rather than a means of realizing an ideal social order (*LDP*, 46; see *CME*, 4:355–56, 377–78). Carlyle's "green flowery world" is a capitalist utopia built with forced labor.

Carlyle's loss of sympathy for the poor makes itself manifest everywhere in *Latter-Day Pamphlets*. In *Past and Present*, he had attacked those who denied their kinship—their "sisterhood"—with the Irish widow, but in *Latter-Day Pamphlets* he denies his kinship with the Chartists arrested by Russell in 1848: "In brotherhood with the base and foolish I, for one, do not mean to live" (*PP*, 151; *LDP*, 66; see 77). In *Past and Present*, he could sympathize with a poor couple guilty of murdering their children for insurance money, arguing that the guilt lay equally with the social system that drove them to this act, but he now attacks those who lament the plight of seamstresses (*PP*, 9–10; *LDP*, 27). Carlyle insists in *Latter-Day Pamphlets* (and later in the 1853 "Nigger Question") that it is the greed of these distressed seamstresses, who have given up good jobs as servants, rather than the greed of employers that is responsible for their poverty. Yet he adduces nothing but anecdotal evidence on behalf of his argument and fails to see, as he might have ten years earlier, that the seamstresses might be justified in rejecting an oppressive servitude.[66]

Significantly, Carlyle holds those with the least power in British domains—women, Irish, and blacks—responsible for its social ills. Moreover, he exploits his own as well as his culture's racial prejudices in order to reinforce his criticisms of the poor and unemployed. Although he denied the charge of racism in *Oliver Cromwell's Letters and Speeches* and the 1853 "Nigger Question," it can be readily demonstrated that he employed racial stereotyping and the premise of racial hierarchy to justify his defense of slavery and his proposals for industrial regiments.

Carlyle's racism is most evident in "The Negro Question," which argues that blacks "have to be servants to those that are born *wiser* than [they], that are born lords of [them]" (*CME*, 4:379). Even after Mill publicly criticized these imputations of racial inferiority—he was quick to point out that Carlyle was treating cultural traits as natural ones—Carlyle continued to insist, in *Latter-Day Pamphlets*, that blacks were slaves by the authority of God (*Essays on Equality*, 92–93; *LDP*,

248–49). "The Nigger Question" did not substantially alter this view. Although he now claimed that he did not "hate the Negro"—and there is no reason to believe he was being insincere—he continued to depict blacks as racially inferior.[67] The problem in discussions of Carlyle's racial attitudes is that it is incorrectly assumed by his defenders that an absence of racial hatred is incompatible with the presence of racial prejudice. Carlyle was not being inconsistent; the claim that one loves one's inferiors is the foundation of paternalism.

Carlyle's prejudice against Celts enabled him to substitute the West Indian blacks of "The Negro/Nigger Question" for the Irish of the projected book on the Irish Question. A letter to Emerson, written just after his 1849 visit to Ireland, reveals how the two groups were related to one another in his mind: "'*Blacklead* these 2 million idle beggars,' I sometimes advised, 'and sell them in Brazil as Niggers,—perhaps Parliament, on sweet constraint, will allow you to advance them to be Niggers!'" (*RWE*, 456). He made it clear elsewhere that he believed he and his Annandale forebears were descended from the Danish rather than the Celtic settlers of Scotland: "The Annandale Scotch . . . are all Danes . . . stalwart Normans: terrible Sea-Kings are now terrible drainers of Morasses, terrible spinners of yarn, coal-borers, removers of mountains. . . . The windy Celts of *Gallo*way meet us, not many miles from this, on the edge of Nithsdale: is it not a considerable blessing to have escaped being born a Celt?" (*CL*, 13:192; see 278–79 and n. 2). Although he recognized that subjection to unjust landlords might be responsible for the development of undesirable cultural traits, none-theless, as early as *Chartism*, he represented the Irish stereotypically as "Immethodic, headlong, violent, mendacious" (*CME*, 4:137). By 1849, in spite of his friendship with and admiration for Gavan Duffy, he had come to consider the majority of Irish as incorrigible beggars, reduced to "deceptive human *swine*" (*RIJ*, 176; see 193).[68]

Carlyle seems to conclude that if the transcendental word cannot persuade the poor to work, it can only be because they are racially incapable of vision. His caricatures of blacks and Irish as well as the impoverished working class insist that they, like Cagliostro, merely eat and drink, that they consume rather than create. In "The Negro/Nigger Question," the blacks of the West Indies loll about eating pump-kin, and in *Latter-Day Pamphlets*, paupers, seamstresses, and the Irish are drunkards who turn down every opportunity to do honest work (e.g., 28, 39–40; see August, xviii–xix). Whereas Carlyle had earlier sought to convert the middle class, he now turned to trying to coerce the working class (*LDP*, 93–94; see *RIJ*, 120; *CME*, 4:355–57, 375–76).

The Carlyle who had once recoiled from the Bucanier morality of the middle class now recoils from the "ape-faces, imp-faces, angry dog-faces, heavy sullen ox-faces" of a monstrous and bestial working class (*LDP*, 55). The rhetoric of *Latter-Day Pamphlets*, as manifested in the passage just cited, dehumanizes the working class, depicting the poor as animals, or even inanimate offal. "Pauperism" becomes "the poisonous dripping from all the sins, and putrid unveracities and godforgetting greedinesses and devil-serving cants and jesuitisms, that exist among us" (158). In spite of the fact that, as Carlyle must have known, the foul odors, slime, ooze, and fetid effluvia to which he repeatedly alludes were the inescapable conditions of life in the poverty-stricken districts of major cities, in the *Pamphlets* he transfers what had once been a revulsion against the putridness of greed to the poison of poverty (27–28, 159, 164, 167).

Carlyle's anger against the working class was rooted in his contradictory desire for a revolution that would complete the Puritan revolution by reestablishing hierarchical authority. Although he had demonstrated in *The French Revolution*, and even in *Oliver Cromwell's Letters and Speeches*, that revolution unleashes anarchy that cannot be controlled except by repression, he had continued to hope that revolution could reestablish authority. The anger of *Latter-Day Pamphlets* manifests his bitter disappointment that the revolutions of 1848 did not bring England a new Cromwell. Whereas in 1789 the French people had risen up and rid themselves of false government, he complained, the people now let themselves be the "dupes" of "Sham-Kings" (12, 11; see 13–14). *Latter-Day Pamphlets* argues for the use of the "whip" to control the rebellious working classes and simultaneously brandishes the whip at them because they have failed to rebel.

This contradiction is most fully evident in the final *Pamphlet*, "Jesuitism," which unexpectedly sides with sansculottism rather than authority. On the face of it, Ignatius Loyola might be one of Carlyle's heroes. At a time when belief was being challenged, Loyola—using the same metaphor Carlyle favored when he conceived the "industrial regiments"—had created a symbolic army to defend the hierarchical authority of the pope against "Sansculottism" (330). Indeed, Carlyle cannot help praising the Jesuits' emphasis on obedience to authority.